IMAGES OF WAR
THE GHETTOS OF NAZI-OCCUPIED POLAND

RARE PHOTOGRAPHS FROM WARTIME ARCHIVES

Ian Baxter

Pen & Sword
MILITARY

First published in Great Britain in 2020 by
PEN & SWORD MILITARY
An imprint of
Pen & Sword Books Ltd
47 Church Street
Barnsley
South Yorkshire
S70 2AS

Copyright © Ian Baxter, 2020

ISBN 978-1-52676-180-4

The right of Ian Baxter to be identified as author of this work has been asserted by him in accordance with the Copyright, Designs and Patents Act 1988.

A CIP catalogue record for this book is available from the British Library.

All rights reserved. No part of this book may be reproduced or transmitted in any form or by any means, electronic or mechanical including photocopying, recording or by any information storage and retrieval system, without permission from the Publisher in writing.

Typeset by Concept, Huddersfield, West Yorkshire HD4 5JL
Printed and bound in India by Replika Press Pvt. Ltd

Pen & Sword Books Limited incorporates the imprints of Atlas, Archaeology, Aviation, Discovery, Family History, Fiction, History, Maritime, Military, Military Classics, Politics, Select, Transport, True Crime, Air World, Frontline Publishing, Leo Cooper, Remember When, Seaforth Publishing, The Praetorian Press, Wharncliffe Local History, Wharncliffe Transport, Wharncliffe True Crime and White Owl.

For a complete list of Pen & Sword titles please contact
PEN & SWORD BOOKS LIMITED
47 Church Street, Barnsley, South Yorkshire S70 2AS, England
E-mail: enquiries@pen-and-sword.co.uk
Website: www.pen-and-sword.co.uk

Contents

Preface **5**

Historical Background **6**

Chapter One
   Ghettoization **7**

Chapter Two
   Life in the Ghettos **27**

Chapter Three
   Liquidation of the Ghettos **55**

Chapter Four
   The Warsaw Uprising **73**

The Aftermath **95**

Appendix I
   List of Polish Ghettos **97**

Appendix II
   Reserve Police Battalion 101 . . . . **127**

The views or opinions expressed in this book and the context in which the images are used do not necessarily reflect the views or policy of, nor imply approval or endorsement by, the United States Holocaust Memorial Museum (USHMM).

About the Author

Ian Baxter is a military historian who specialises in German twentieth-century military history. He has written more than fifty books including *Poland – The Eighteen Day Victory March*, *Panzers In North Africa*, *The Ardennes Offensive*, *The Western Campaign*, *The 12th SS Panzer-Division Hitlerjugend*, *The Waffen-SS on the Western Front*, *The Waffen-SS on the Eastern Front*, *The Red Army at Stalingrad*, *Elite German Forces of World War II*, *Armoured Warfare*, *German Tanks of War*, *Blitzkrieg*, *Panzer-Divisions at War*, *Hitler's Panzers*, *German Armoured Vehicles of World War Two*, *Last Two Years of the Waffen-SS at War*, *German Soldier Uniforms and Insignia*, *German Guns of the Third Reich*, *Defeat to Retreat: The Last Years of the German Army At War 1943–45*, *Operation Bagration – the Destruction of Army Group Centre*, *German Guns of the Third Reich*, *Rommel and the Afrika Korps*, *U-Boat War*, and most recently *The Sixth Army and the Road to Stalingrad*. He has written over a hundred articles including 'Last days of Hitler', 'Wolf's Lair', 'The Story of the V1 and V2 Rocket Programme', 'Secret Aircraft of World War Two', 'Rommel at Tobruk', 'Hitler's War With his Generals', 'Secret British Plans to Assassinate Hitler', 'The SS at Arnhem', 'Hitlerjugend', 'Battle of Caen 1944', 'Gebirgsjäger at War', 'Panzer Crews', 'Hitlerjugend Guerrillas', 'Last Battles in the East', 'The Battle of Berlin', and many more. He has also reviewed numerous military studies for publication, supplied thousands of photographs and important documents to various publishers and film production companies worldwide, and lectures to various schools, colleges and universities throughout the United Kingdom and the Republic of Ireland.

Preface

It was my intention to write no more about the treatment of the Jews by the Nazis: I believed there were already enough books on the subject. It was my 12-year-old son Felix who suggested I write about the ghettos. I looked into the idea and found he was right: there was room for another book, especially one with pictures and captions. The Holocaust has placed an indelible mark upon the twentieth century and on our consciousness. As I researched I became increasingly interested in how the Nazi government planned to control the Jewish population, forcing them to live in special restricted sections of towns.

The Nazi leadership in Berlin saw the ghettos as a provisional measure to control and segregate Jews while they deliberated on their fate. Their decision was to transport them to various labour or death camps around Europe where almost all of them would die.

There were around a thousand ghettos in Europe during the early period of the war, but my focus in the book was mainly on the Polish ghettos of Warsaw, Łódź, and Kraków. For these I was able to find sufficient material including many images, the bulk of which I have obtained from the United States Holocaust Memorial Museum (USHMM).

The photographs in this book were mostly taken by German soldiers with a passion for photography who were stationed in the surrounding towns and cities and given access to the ghettos. For instance, Willy Georg, radio operator: while stationed in Warsaw he supplemented his income by taking pictures of his comrades, and during the summer of 1941 he was issued a pass by one of his officers and given instructions to enter the ghetto and bring back photos of what he saw.

Sergeant Heinrich Joest was also stationed in Warsaw in 1941. With his Rolleiflex camera he was given permission to enter the ghetto and in just one day he shot 140 images of life there, some of which are revealed in this book.

There is also a collection of unique colour slides taken by Walter Genewein. Genewein was head of the Łódź ghetto economy serving under Hans Biebow. He was a keen amateur photographer, and with his camera took chilling photographs of life in the Łódź ghetto including disturbing photos of Jews being prepared for transportation to labour or death camps.

I hope that this book will become a valuable addition to Holocaust studies, and we all hope that we never have to encounter such an abhorrent regime as that of the Nazis ever again.

Historical Background

With Adolf Hitler's swift victory over Poland in September 1939 the Germans acquired territory with a population of 20 million, of whom 17 million were Polish and 675,000 were German. His plan had always been to clear the Poles and Jews from these territories and replace them with German settlers. What followed was a period of unrestrained terror in Poland, particularly in the incorporated territories. The areas not incorporated contained a population of some 11 million. These included the provinces of Lublin and parts of Warsaw and Kraków. Initially they were collectively termed the 'General Government of the Occupied Polish Areas' and in 1940 were renamed the 'General Government'. This large area was used as the dumping ground for all those deemed undesirable and enemies of the state. It was here that the first Poles and Jews were deported in their thousands.

During the first cold months of 1940 the General Government forced thousands of homeless and penniless people into an already overpopulated area. In their place came thousands of ethnic Germans, all of whom had to be provided with suitable housing. The scale of the relocation was enormous and chaotic.

By the end of January the immense problems of simultaneously attempting to relocate Poles, Jews and ethnic Germans had become such an administrative nightmare that it was agreed that all Jews should be forced to live in ghettos. The first ghetto was established on 8 October 1939 at Piotrkow Trybunalski, just days after the defeat of Poland. Two months later another had been erected in Tuliszkow. The Nazis saw that the ghettos would not only relieve the burden of the resettlement programme, but it was also a way of temporarily getting rid of the Jewish problem. The Nazis hated and feared the Jews, and believed that Eastern Jews in particular were carriers of disease; to isolate them in ghettos was deemed immediately practicable. Plans were put into practice across the General Government to create an extensive network of ghettos, while the rest of the country outside these isolated areas continued to endure harsh Nazi policies.

Chapter One

Ghettoization

Designated areas of larger Polish cities were outlined in a massive programme of ghettoization. The programme was headed by Hans Frank who became Governor General of the occupied Polish territories with responsibility for the administration of the General Government. It was he who put into action the segregation of the Jews and their 'ghettoization'.

Frank's plan was to uproot all Polish Jews from their homes and businesses through compulsory expulsions. Entire Jewish communities were to be deported by train from their places of origin into special closed-off zones using Order Police Battalions. These battalions were subordinated to the SS and deployed specifically in army group rear areas and territories under German civilian administration. The police units were given strict orders to target the civilian population throughout the General Government and specifically to carry out the expulsion of Poles from the Reichsgau Wartheland under the new Lebensraum policies. They were told to be as brutal as necessary to expedite what they referred to as 'Resettlement Actions'.

The Police Battalions, often supported by army units, moved into selected areas and removed the local population from their flats and houses, confiscating them. These areas were then marked off to become separated from the rest of society.

Between late 1939 and 1940 there were also expulsions from German-occupied 'Greater Poland'. Some 680,000 Poles were expelled from the city of Poznań in Reichsgau Wartheland alone, of whom approximately 70,000 were moved into the General Government. These deportations were conducted under the leadership of SS-Obergruppenführer Wilhelm Koppe.

The first deportations of the Jewish community into the newly-created ghetto system began in October 1939. All Jewish homes and businesses were vacated through forcible expulsions in a very short period of time. On the day of their removal notice, Jews received orders to present themselves at special assembly points so that they could be 'evacuated further east'. Each person was issued with an evacuation number – a number which would give the authorities details of where they would be transported. So as not to create panic, the deportees were allowed to take 50kg of luggage. They also had to pay for their own railway tickets.

The first major transports began with the removal of some 70,000 to 80,000 Jews from Ostrava district in Moravia (now in eastern Czech Republic) and in Katowice district in the recently annexed portion of Poland. SS-Obersturmführer Adolf Eichmann was tasked with managing the logistics of the mass deportation of Jews to the ghettos from these areas, and later to the extermination camps. His priority in 1939 was to remove Jews from the conquered territory of Greater Poland and transport them into the General Government economically and with minimal disruption to Germany's ongoing military operations. By the end of 1941 some 3.5 million Polish Jews had been segregated and ghettoized by Eichmann in his massive deportation action involving the use of hundreds of freight trains.

In October 1941 the first transports of German Jews were sent by rail to either labour camps in Poland or the General Government to be ghettoized. The freight cars (*Güterwagen*) were packed with 150 deportees, although 50 was the number initially proposed by deportation regulations. There was no food or water. An average transport took four days. Many died from hunger or exposure to the elements, and inadequate ventilation resulted in many deaths from suffocation. Often when the trains arrived at their destination and the doors were opened, everyone was dead.

Those that had survived the journey were removed from the trains under armed guard and either marched on foot or transported by vehicle to the ghetto. Even as they arrived inside the ghetto, many still believed this was only a stopover on the way to their new lives further east. They had no idea that they would soon see their ghettos destroyed, often barbarically, and that they would be forced into nearby forests or fields to be murdered, or be transported either to labour camps or death camps around Europe.

(**Opposite, above**) German soldiers beat Polish Jews in the vicinity of Łódź during the invasion of Poland. The persecution of the Jews of Poland began almost immediately after the German invasion. *(USHMM: Mary Jane Farley)*

(**Opposite, below**) Hans Biebow, German head of the Łódź ghetto administration, at his desk. Under his administration, and with the help of Adolf Eichmann, he moved 164,000 Jews to Poland's second largest city, Łódź. Communication between the ghetto inhabitants and the outside world was completely cut off and the supply of food was severely limited, with the result that many of the inhabitants of the ghetto would starve to death. He was also responsible for assisting the Gestapo and other police authorities rounding up Jews during deportations. *(USHMM: Robert Abrams)*

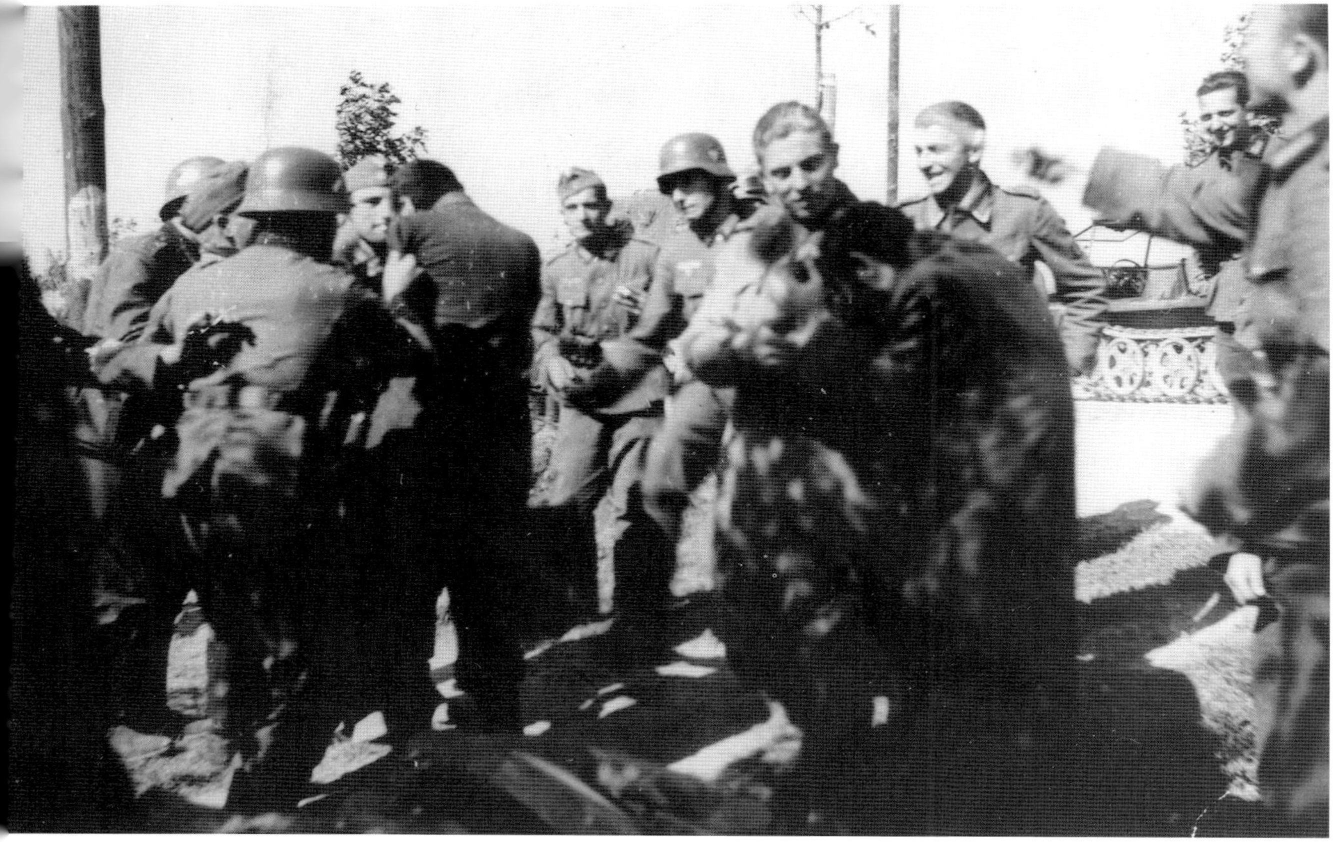

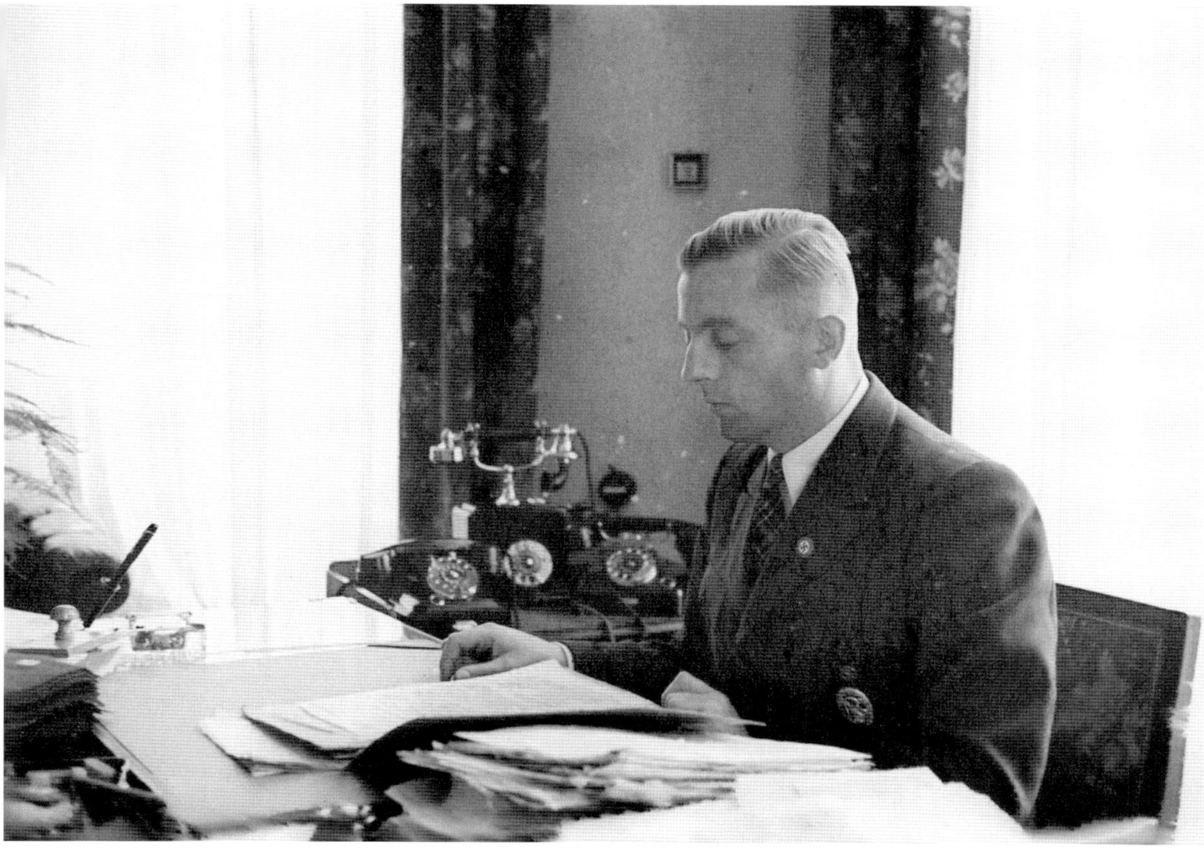

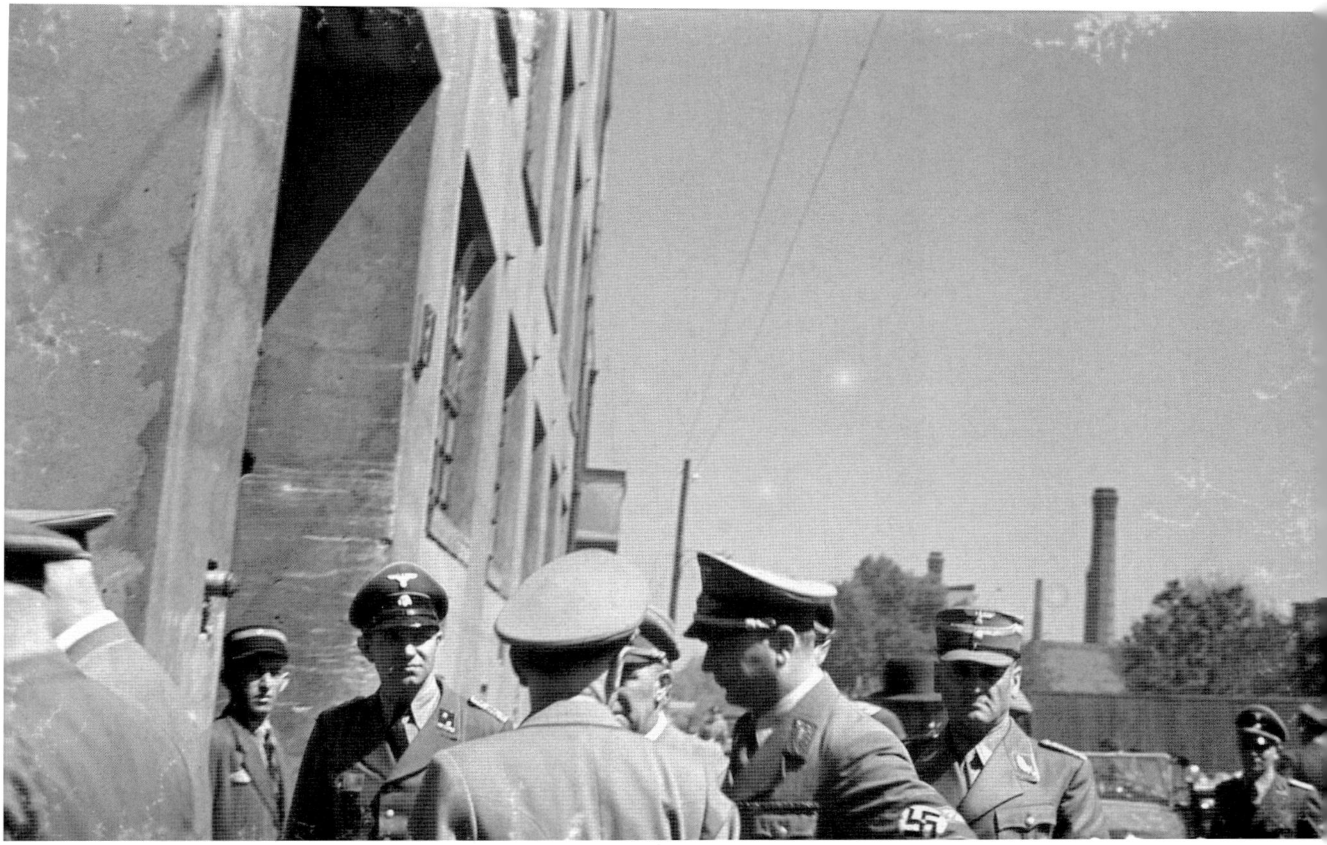

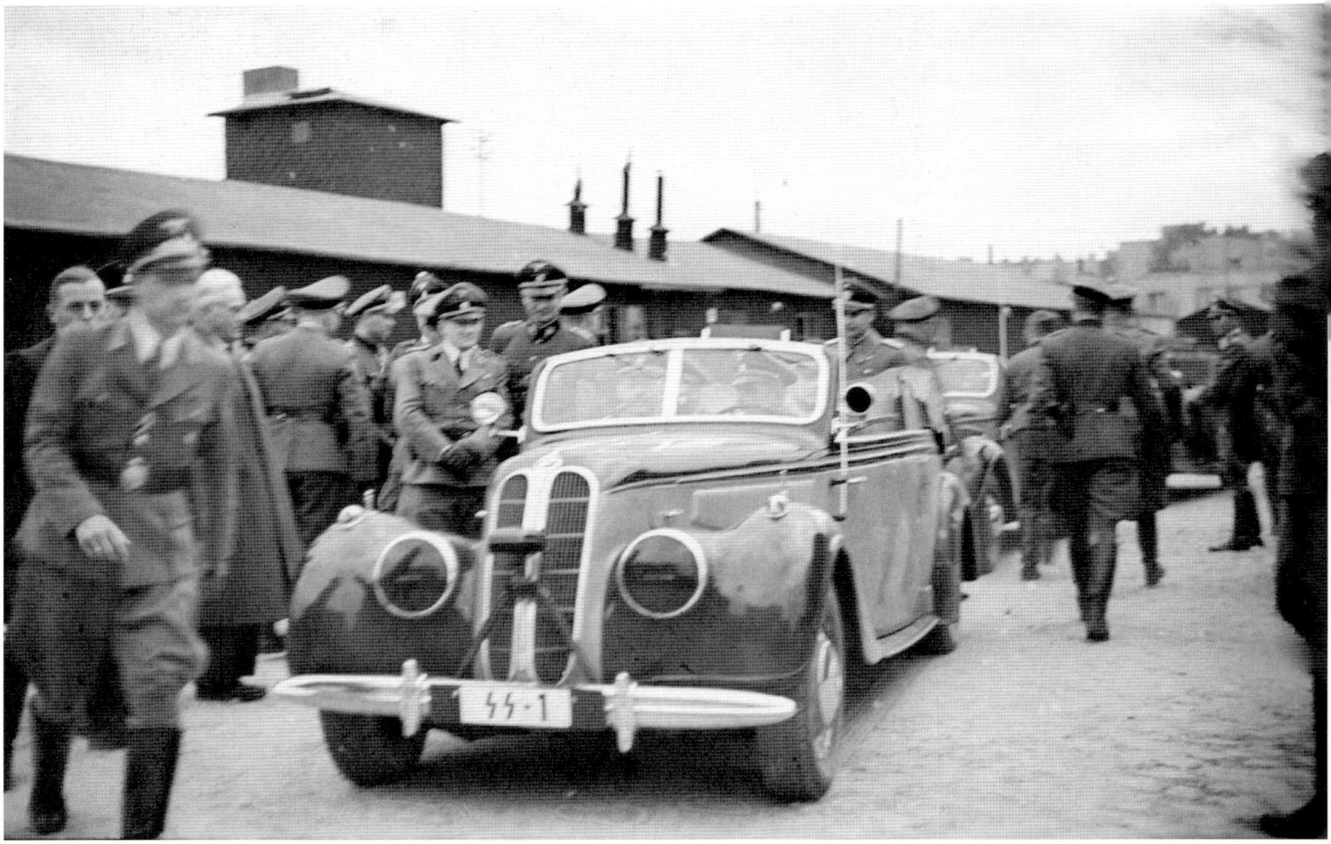

(**Opposite, above**) Gauleiters attend a meeting in the Łódź ghetto in 1941. Pictured is Arthur Greiser and Wilhelm Frick. Greiser was *Reichsstatthalter* (Reich governor) of the German-occupied territory of Wartheland and was one of those primarily responsible for organising the transportation from his domain to the ghettos in Poland and later responsible for the Jews being moved to their deaths in the concentration camps. Frick was Protector of Bohemia and Moravia and was a ruthless individual. He assisted in the transportation of Jews from the Czech region to the concentration camps. (*USHMM: Robert Abrams*)

(**Opposite, below**) An official visit of Heinrich Himmler to the Łódź ghetto. Mordechai Chaim Rumkowski, head of the Jewish council, greets the Nazi officials. Standing to the right of the car is Karl Wolff, Chief of Personal Staff to Himmler. He was responsible for ordering the deportation of all male Jews of Polish nationality and their families to the ghettos. Later in 1942 he oversaw the liquidation of the Warsaw ghetto and the Jews' mass extermination. (*USHMM: Robert Abrams*)

(**Above**) Hans Biebow stands next to a car in a street in the Łódź ghetto. (*USHMM: Robert Abrams*)

Hans Biebow, Nazi administrator of the Łódź ghetto, poses in front of a car. *(USHMM: Robert Abrams)*

Hans Biebow oversees the running of the ghetto. He can be seen standing at a Jewish market. *(USHMM: Robert Abrams)*

This photograph shows deportees arriving by train at the Radogoszcz station in Marysin, destined for the Łódź ghetto. They were unloaded off these trains and marched in columns to the ghetto. Often they brought small bundles of belongings with them. (USHMM: Robert Abrams)

Jews who are being forced to relocate to the Kraków ghetto in 1940 can be seen moving their belongings in carts and horse-drawn wagons across a bridge over the Vistula. (USHMM: Zydowski Instytut Historyczny imienia Emanuela R'ngelbluma)

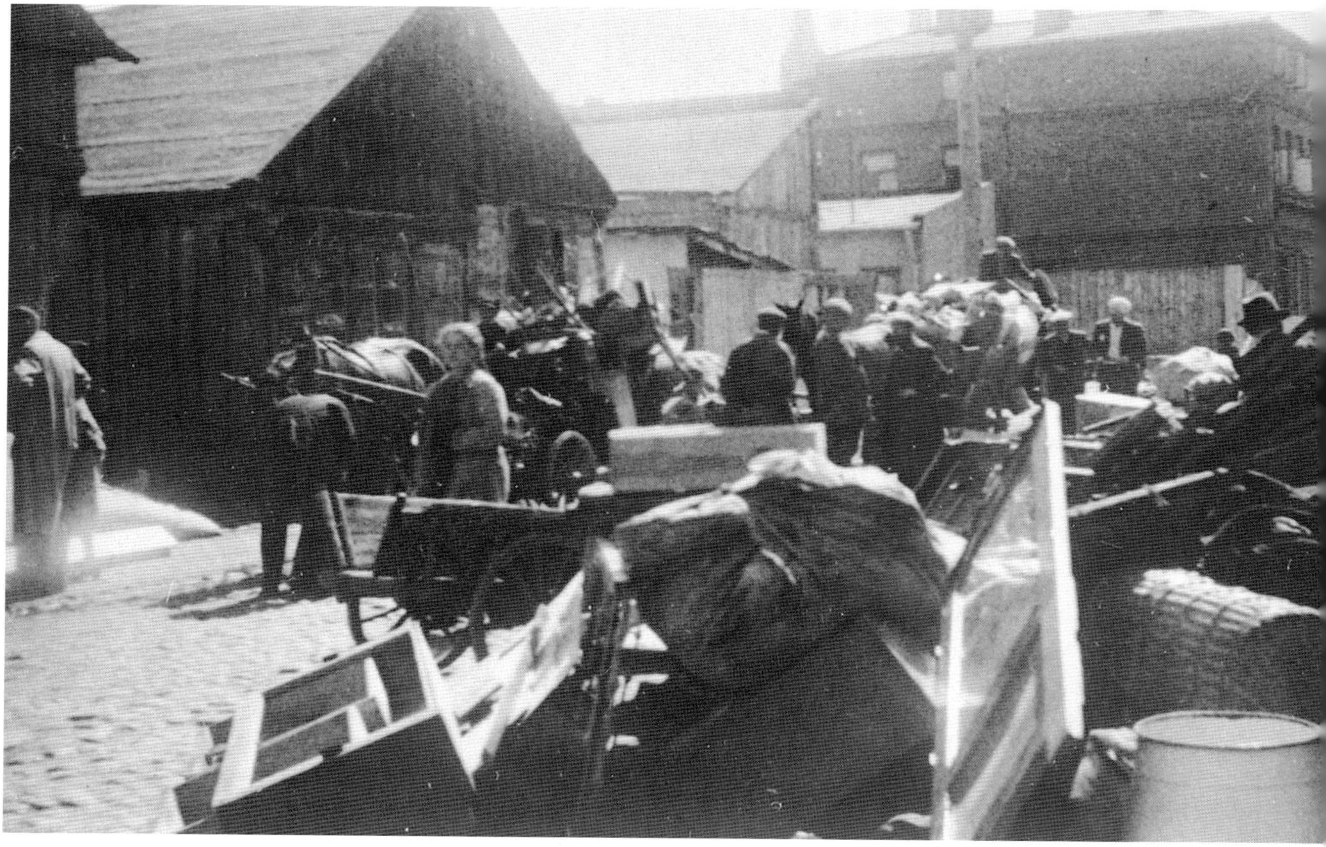

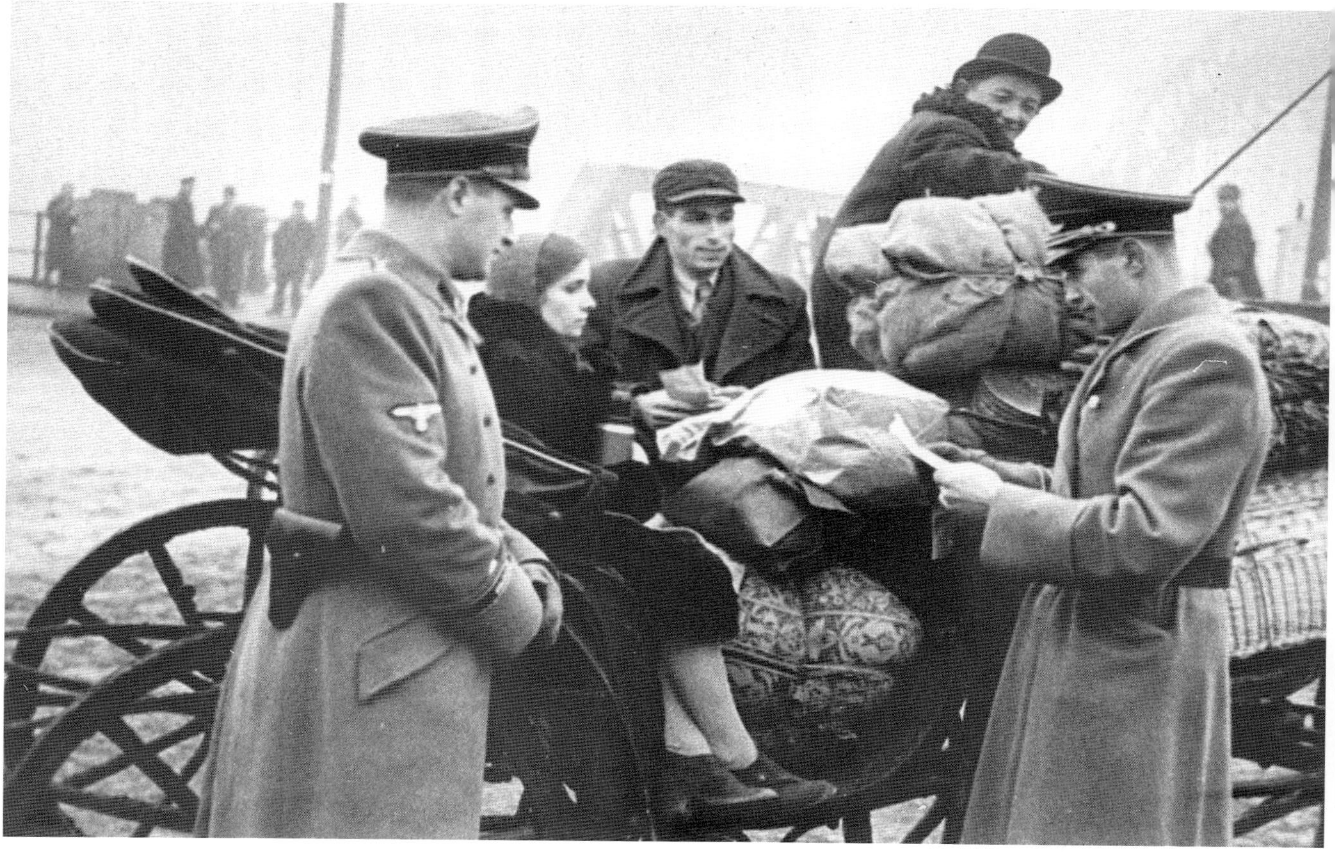

(**Opposite, above**) Jews move their belongings to the Kutno ghetto. More than 7,000 were crowded into the grounds of the factory, several buildings of which had been bombed, forcing many of the new tenants to make outdoor living arrangements. The Germans surrounded the area with barbed wire and watchtowers.
(USHMM: Instytut Pamieci Narodowej)

(**Opposite, below**) A German officer checks the papers of Jews moving into the Kraków ghetto.
(USHMM: Archiwum Panstwowe w Krakówie)

(**Above**) Jews haul their belongings into the Łódź ghetto in 1940. (USHMM: Moshe Zilbar)

Two German regulars interrogate a bearded Polish Jew. *(USHMM: Leonard Lauder)*

Horse-drawn wagons along Kosciuszko Street in Belchatow during the relocation of Jews to the ghetto. Half of the population of the town was Jewish. The ghetto operated until August 1942 when it was liquidated. The occupants were sent either to the Łódź ghetto or directly to the Chełmno concentration camp. (*USHMM: County Court of Belchatow*)

German troops supervise a column of (probably Polish) Jews marching by the side of a road in a forced resettlement action. These Jews would be relocated to a ghetto. (*USHMM: Michael O'Hara*)

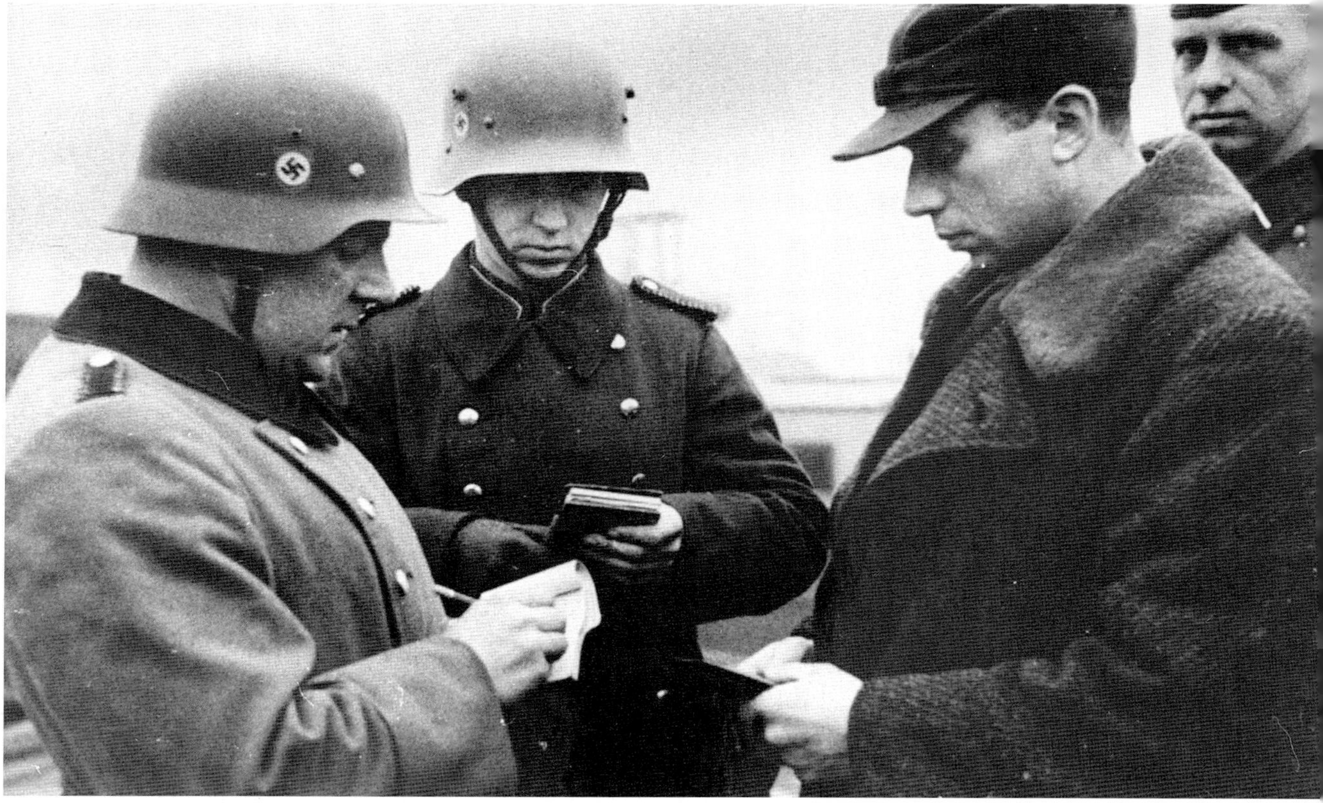

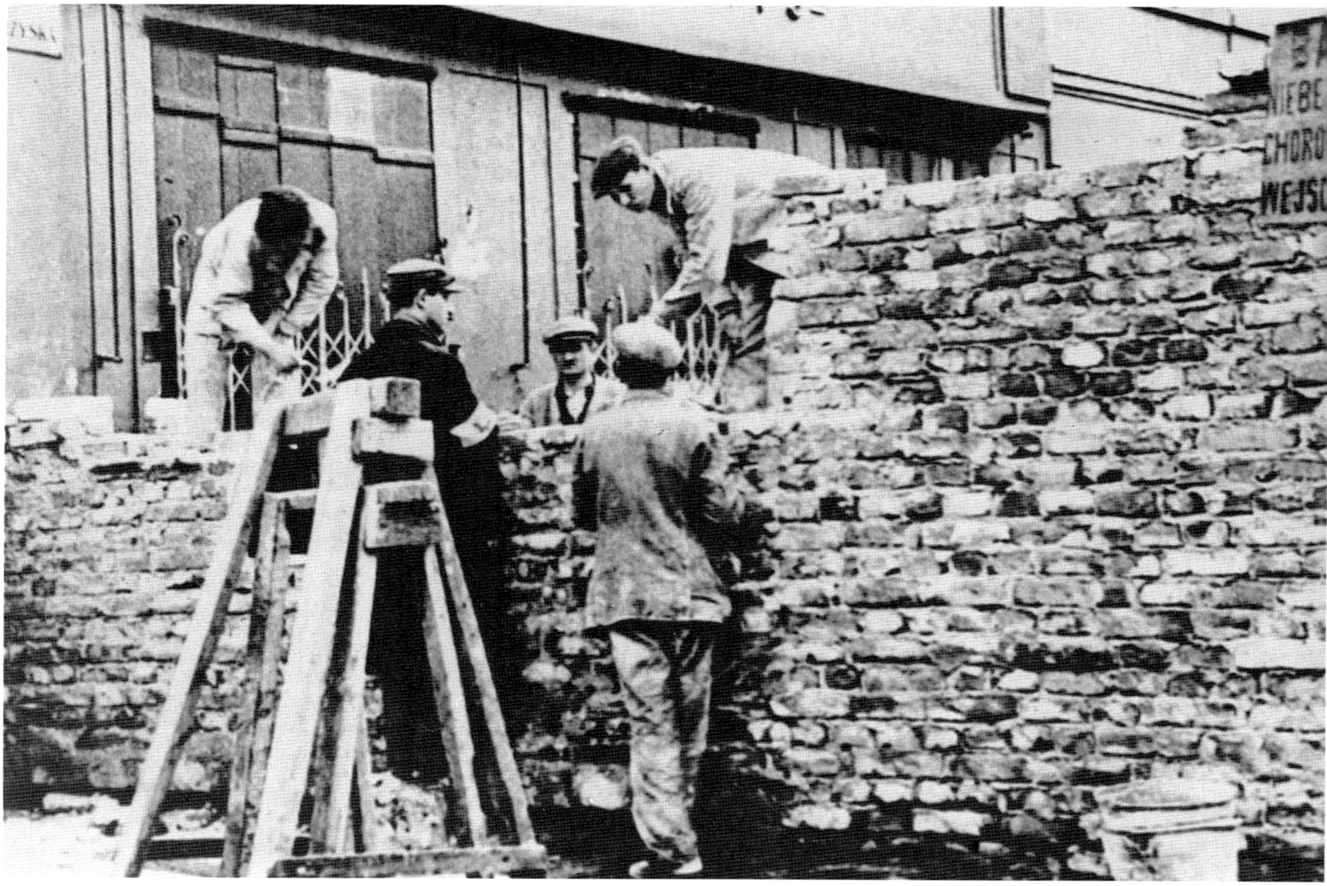
NIEBE
CHORO
WEJSC

(**Opposite, above**) German police check the identification papers of a Jew in the streets of Kraków, more than likely before the establishment of the Kraków ghetto in March 1941. The ghetto was to be set up in the Jewish quarter in Pódgorze, a suburb of the city. All non-Jewish residents of the area were required to relocate in other districts of the city by 20 March 1941. (*USHMM: Archiwum Panstwowe w Krakówie*)

(**Opposite, below**) Polish and Jewish labourers construct a section of the wall that separated the Warsaw ghetto from the rest of the city. On the orders of Warsaw District Governor Ludwig Fischer, construction of the ghetto wall began on 1 April 1940. The wall would completely encircle the ghetto and segregate the inhabitants from the inhabitants of Warsaw. By 16 October 1940 the ghetto was officially in operation and imprisoned 375,000 to 400,000 Jews. (*USHMM: Leopold Page Photographic Collection*)

(**Above**) Jews are forced to construct the wall around the newly erected Kraków ghetto. Many of these walls contained brick panels in the shape of tombstones, which appealed to the sadistic German authorities overseeing the ghetto operation. All windows and doors that opened onto the 'Aryan' side were ordered to be bricked up. There were four main entrances that allowed traffic to pass in and out. (*USHMM: Instytut Pamieci Narodowej*)

(**Above**) Polish labourers seal off the doors and windows of buildings on the outer border of the Kraków ghetto. (*USHMM: Instytut Pamieci Narodowej*)

(**Opposite, above**) Jewish workers are forced to construct the wall around the Kraków ghetto. The ghetto district comprised 30 streets and 320 residential buildings. When first formed it was populated by some 16,000 Jews. (*USHMM: Instytut Pamieci Narodowej*)

(**Opposite, below**) Two German soldiers pose at the entrance to an unidentified ghetto in Poland. This photograph was more than likely taken between 1940 and 1941 when most of the Polish ghettos across the General Government were being constructed. (*USHMM: Harry Lore*)

JUDISCHES WOHNGEBIET
BETRETEN durch DEUTSCHE und POLEN VERBOTEN
Der Kreishauptmann

DZIELNICA ŻYDOWSKA
NIEMCOM i POLAKOM WSTĘP WZBRONIONY
Der Kreishauptmann

(**Above**) Jewish police open the gates to a street that divides the Warsaw ghetto. Overhead, a pedestrian bridge spans the two sections of the ghetto. This photograph is one of a series of photographs taken by an unidentified German soldier in 1942. *(USHMM: Simon Adelman)*

(**Opposite**) Two photographs taken by a member of Police Battalion 101, one showing the guards from the battalion guarding the perimeter of the Łódź ghetto during the night, the other showing just the perimeter area and one of the guard sentry boxes. The duties of this battalion consisted of controlling civilian populations of the conquered or 'colonised countries' to assist the Einsatzgruppen murder squads as they advanced through Russia murdering Jews and elements they considered undesirable to the Reich. They also rounded up Jews and deported them to the ghettos, and guarded them. On 28 November 1940 the police battalion was redeployed to guard the perimeter of the Łódź ghetto. Later during the liquidation of the ghetto system across the General Government in 1942 they were responsible for removing the Jews, supporting the operations to send them to labour or death camps, and murdering them in wholesale executions in forests and fields. *(USHMM: Michael O'Hara)*

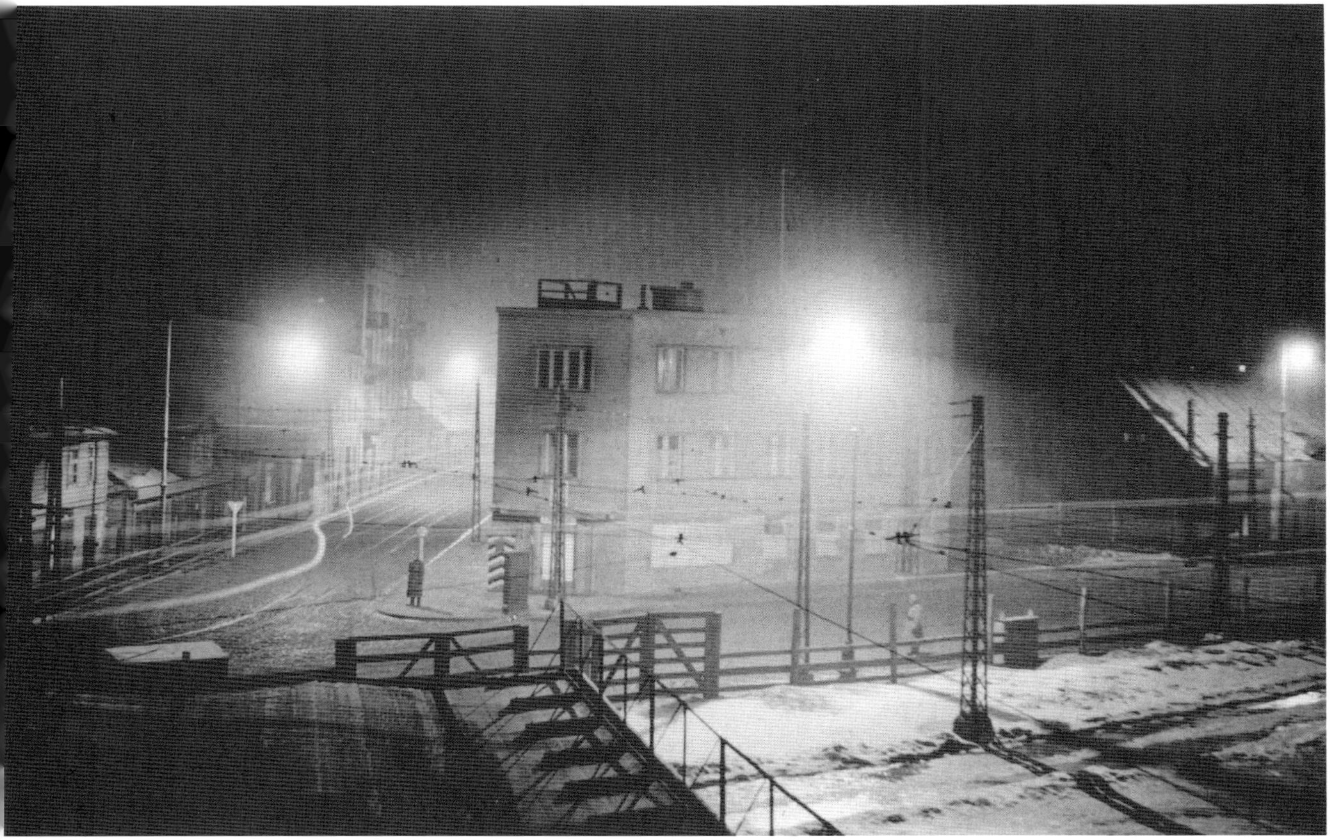

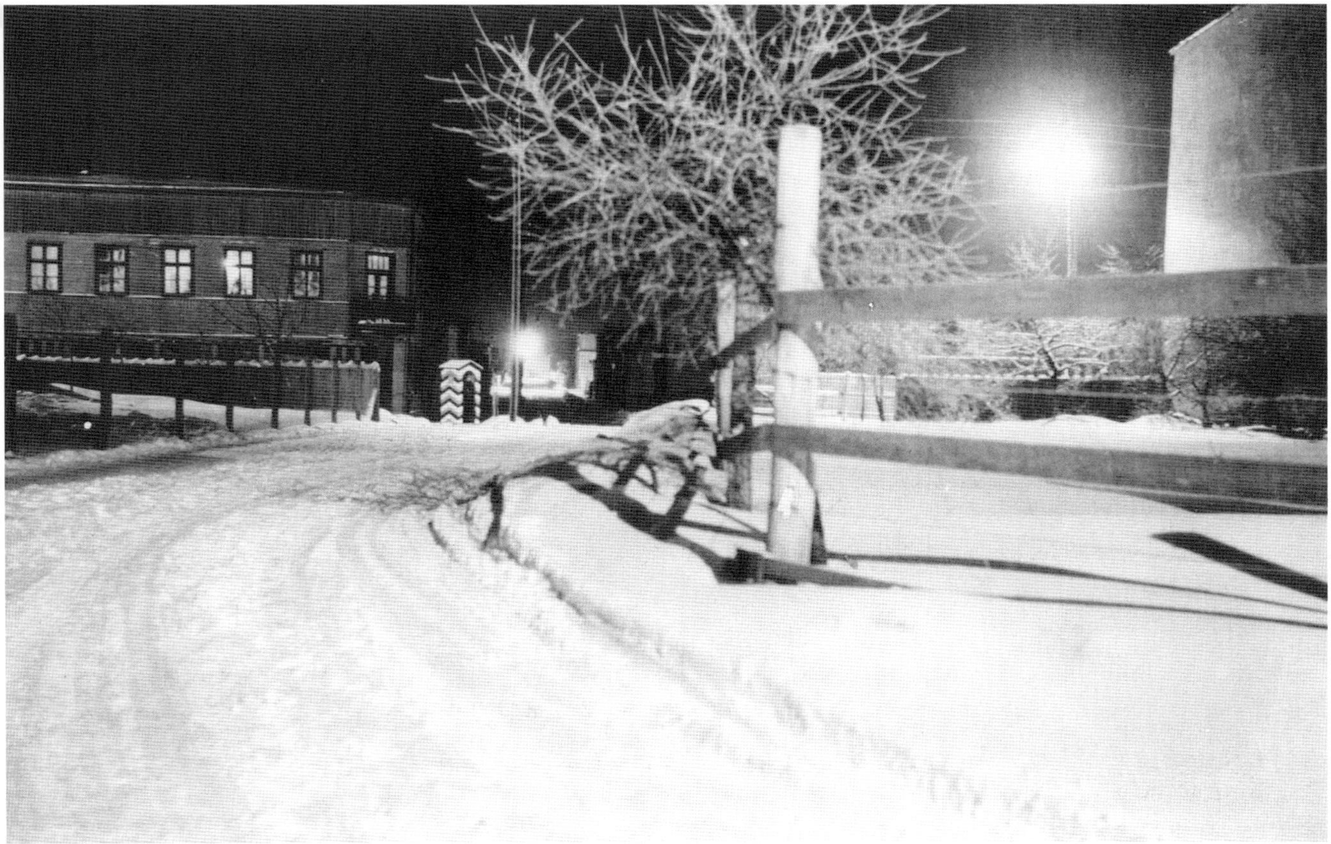

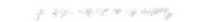

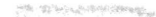

Taken in July 1941, this shows Symche Spira, the senior officer of the Kraków ghetto police (*Ordnungsdienst*) straightening the cap of one of his men during roll call. Members of the Ordnungsdienst in Kraków wore a uniform with an armband with 'Ordnungsdienst' written in Hebrew. The badges were made in the shape of the Star of David surrounding an oval that gave the officer's number. (*USHMM: Raphael Aronson*)

Postcard from the Łódź ghetto showing the entrance and a sign forbidding entrance to non-Jews. (*USHMM: Antonii Marianowicz*)

View of Łódź ghetto residents climbing the staircase to cross one of the pedestrian bridges. The Yiddish inscription on the back of the photo reads, 'The ghetto through the bridge on Marynarska Street via Aleksandrov Street – Fayfer's Alley.' *(USHMM: Abram Zelig)*

Chapter Two

Life in the Ghetto

Typically during the early part of the war there were two types of ghettos. The first was open, with no walls or fences, and the other was closed, or sealed. The latter were surrounded by brick walls, fences or barbed wire stretched between posts. Jews were not allowed to live in any other areas under the threat of punishment or death.

To prevent unauthorised contact between the Jewish and non-Jewish populations, German Order Police battalions were assigned to patrol the perimeter of these new ghettos. Within each ghetto, a Jewish Ghetto Police unit was formed to ensure that no-one tried to escape. One such battalion was Reserve Police Battalion 101. While they patrolled the perimeters of the ghettos, internal security was undertaken by the SS, SD (Security Service), and the Criminal Police, in conjunction with the Jewish ghetto administration.

The Jewish ghetto administration was known as the *Judenräte*. The role of the *Judenräte* was primarily to enforce the Nazis' anti-Jewish regulations. They included rabbis and other influential people of the Jewish community. They were responsible for the internal administration of the ghettos, which was an easy way for the Nazi occupiers to keep control.

In the ghetto a workforce was established to erect brick walls, fences, barbed wire and sometimes bridges to connect one part of a ghetto to another. This was to ensure that the inhabitants of the ghetto would have no interaction with anyone outside its boundaries.

The *Judenräte* also managed its Ghetto Police unit. The Jewish Police, as they were known by the Jews, were responsible for a multitude of tasks. Chiefly to assist the German police guarding the ghetto wall and gates, they were also in charge of distributing food rations, and welfare duties such as aiding the poor. They collected personal belongings, valuables, and accompanied labour battalions that worked outside the ghetto. They also participated in the round-ups for deportations.

Once the Jews entered the ghetto they were ordered to wear identifying badges or armbands with a yellow Star of David. Many strict rules were imposed that were grudgingly implemented by the *Judenräte*. Those caught outside the ghetto could be shot on sight. Contact with people who lived outside the boundaries of the ghetto was forbidden.

All were entirely dependent on the German authorities for food, medicine and other supplies. All who entered the ghetto were sent to specific dwellings to live. Jews could at a moment's notice be instructed to vacate their living quarters and be transferred to another ghetto or house.

Inside the ghetto huge numbers of bewildered, frightened, anxious families were forced into these crowded areas. Often several families shared one house. In the Warsaw ghetto an average of seven people shared a room. The conditions inside the houses were squalid, and due to the lack of running water and sanitation, disease became widespread. Epidemics of infectious disease became a major feature of life. Food was in short supply to the point of starvation. Medical supplies were almost non-existent. Conditions were so bad in the Łódź ghetto that some 43,000 people died. In the Warsaw ghetto 76,000 deaths had been recorded before July 1942.

Polish people living outside the ghetto often went to great lengths to smuggle food into the ghetto. If caught, they faced execution. A black market in food, clothing and medical supplies thrived within the ghetto, with individuals exchanging what possessions they had.

As the ghettos became more established, the German authorities began various business enterprises, often for the war effort, using the inhabitants for forced labour, anything from construction, wood or metal work, to producing clothes. Work was often for long hours under brutal conditions, but for some it offered temporary relief from the hardships of the ghetto. It also gave the workers additional rations and the chance to smuggle in more food or rationed goods.

Life for the Jews in the ghetto was a battle survival. They had no idea that they were destined to lose this battle, as the Nazi plan to eradicate them became a policy.

A member of Reserve Police Battalion 101 German Order Police [*Ordnungspolizei* or *Orpo*] poses at the entrance of Guard Post 5 in the Łódź ghetto. The battalion was divided into three companies, each of approximately 140 men when at full strength. Each company was divided into three platoons with each platoon divided into four squads. It played a central role in the implementation of the 'final solution of the Jewish question' in the Warthegau area. (*USHMM: Michael O'Hara*)

Polizei-
Bataillon 101

112. SS-Standarte

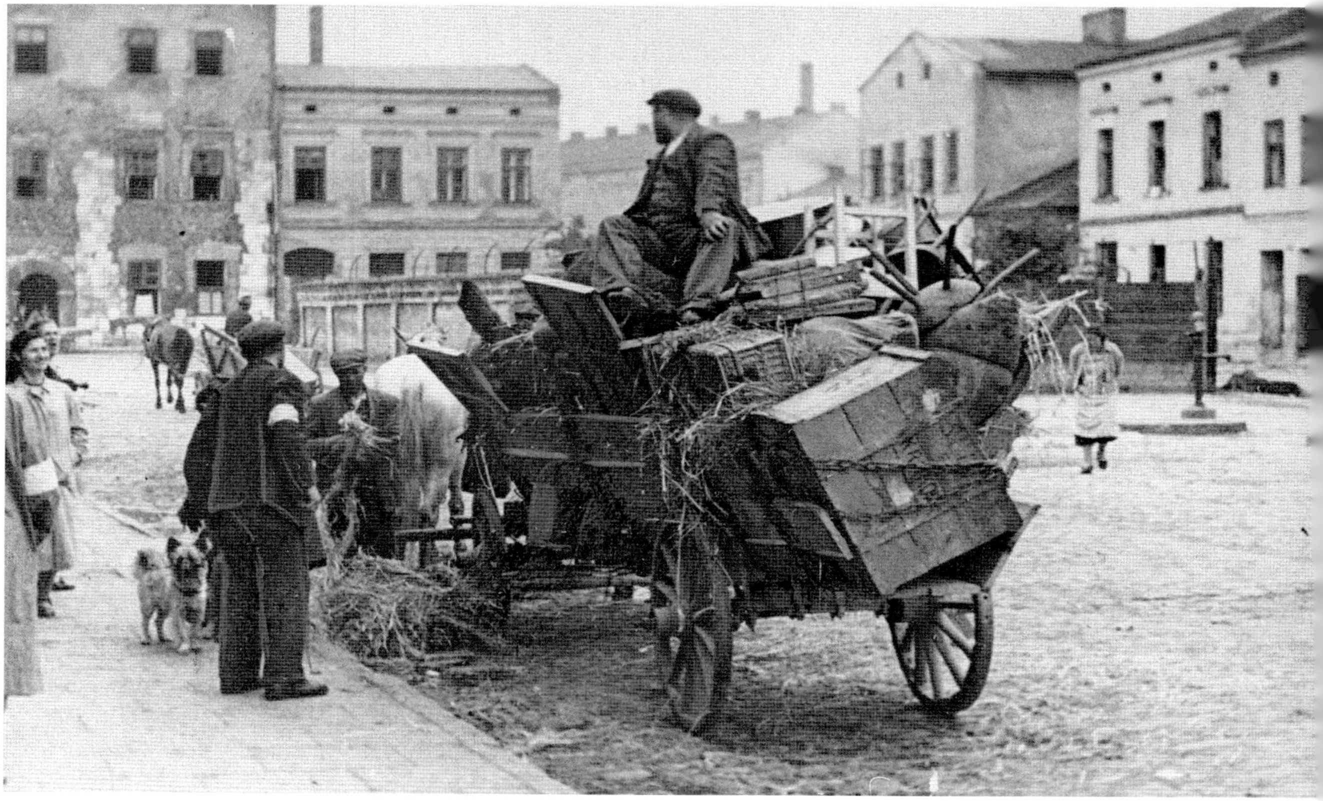

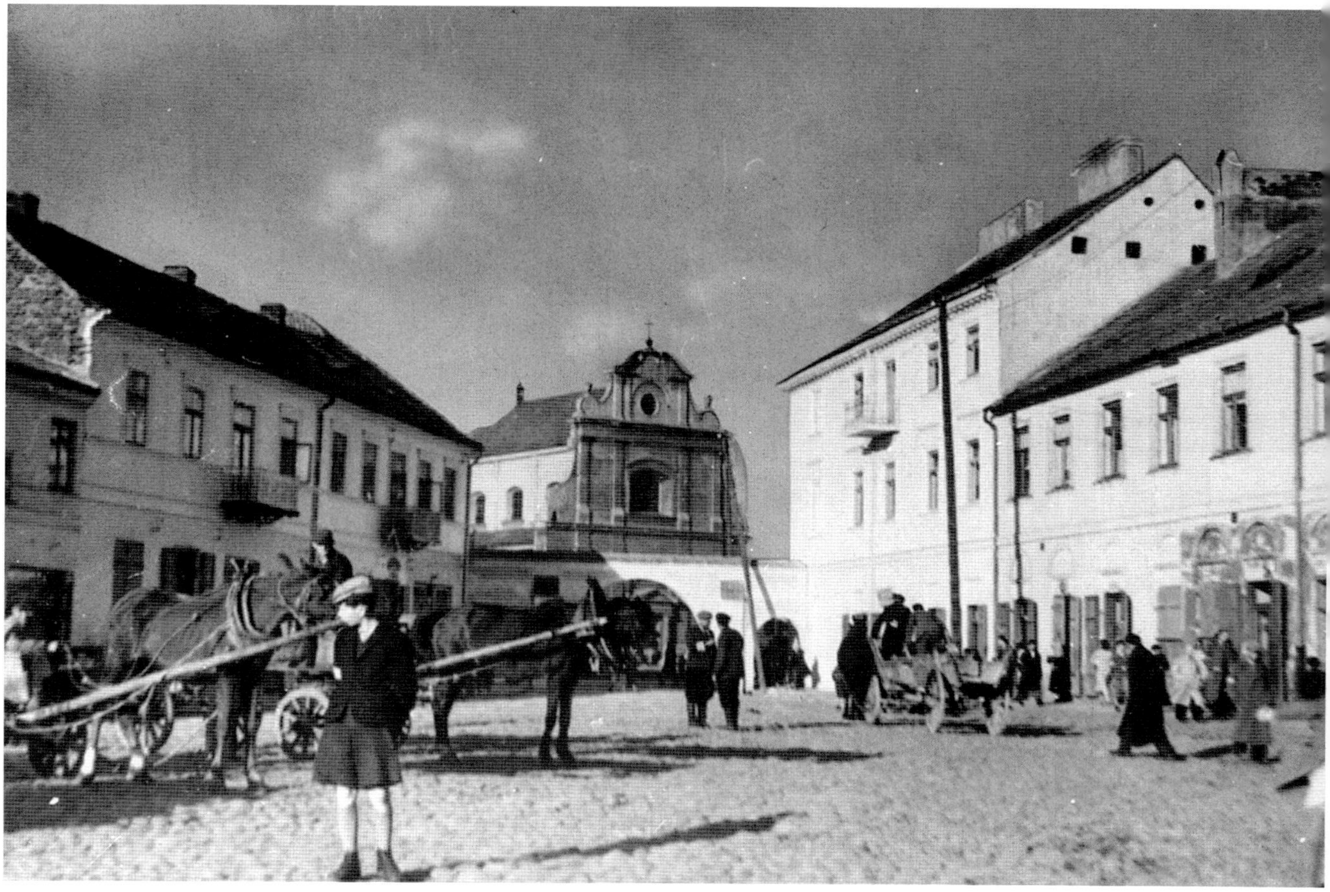

(**Opposite, above**) Forced to relocate to the Kraków ghetto, Jews move their belongings in horse-drawn wagons. (*USHMM: Instytut Pamieci Narodowej*)

(**Above**) At the main gate to the Krzemieniec ghetto, Jewish children polish the boots of Jewish policemen as German soldiers look on. At the end of January 1942 the ghetto was established and by 1 March was closed off from the rest of the city. In the summer of 1942 a liquidation action began, which meant removing and murdering 19,000 of the inhabitants. (*USHMM: Instytut Pamieci Narodowej*)

(**Opposite, below**) View of the main square of the ghetto in Radom. Some 33,000 Polish Jews were contained in the ghetto. Most of it was not closed but consisted of barriers between buildings. Each exit was guarded by Jewish and Polish Police. (*USHMM: Instytut Pamieci Narodowej*)

(**Above**) This photograph was taken in September 1941 and shows the inhabitants of the Warsaw ghetto selling clothing to Polish customers at an open air market. (*USHMM: Guenther Schwarberg*)

(**Opposite, above**) Jews move along a crowded street in the Warsaw ghetto. The German authorities did nothing to alleviate the shortages of food and medical supplies in the ghetto and conditions within it were appalling. (*USHMM: Simon Adelman*)

(**Opposite, below**) Jews purchase produce from street vendors in the Warsaw ghetto. This photograph was one of a number of images taken by a German soldier named Willy Georg. Georg was posted to Warsaw with his unit as a radio operator, and during the summer of 1941 supplemented his income by taking pictures of his comrades. He was issued a pass by one of his officers and instructed to enter the enclosed ghetto and bring back photos of what he saw. (*USHMM: Rafael Scharf*)

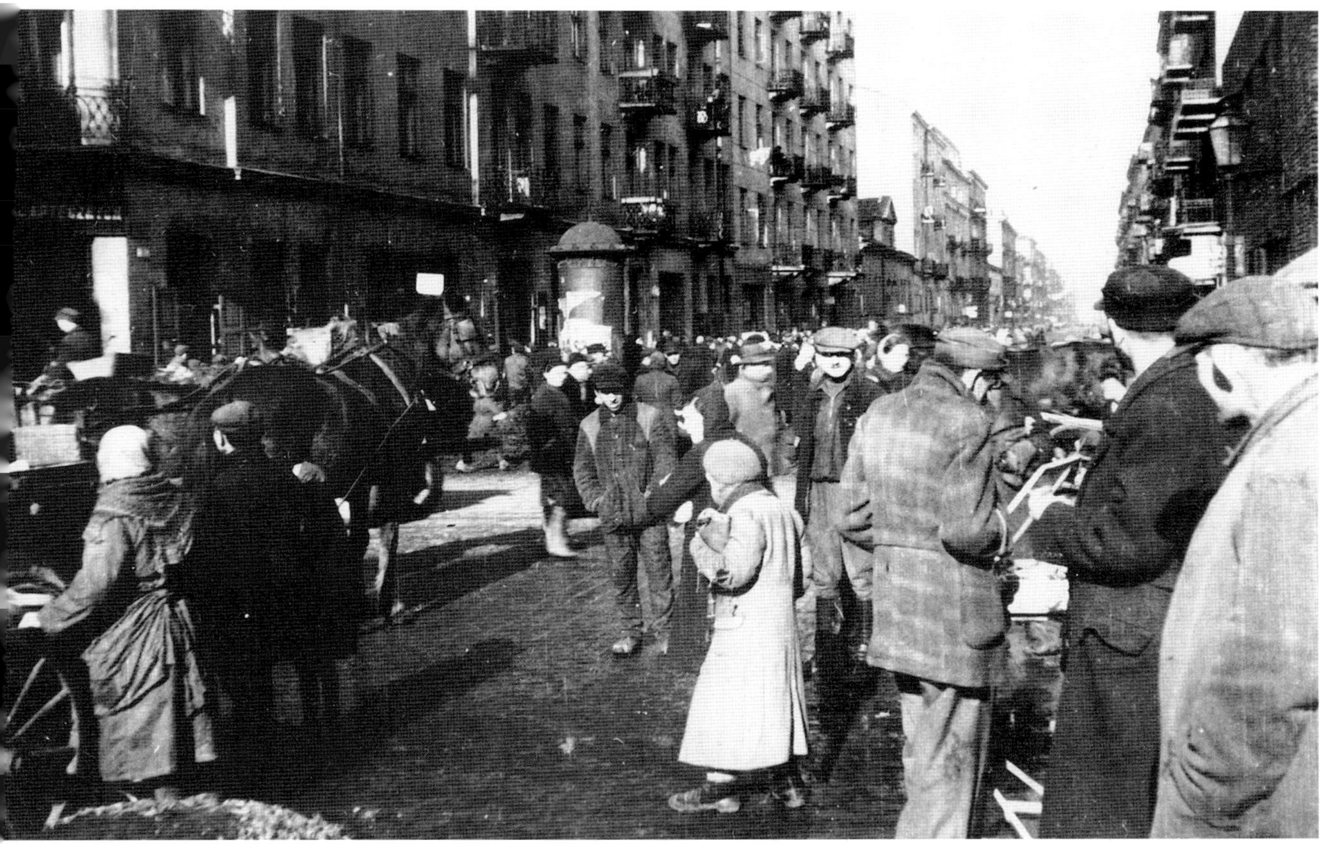

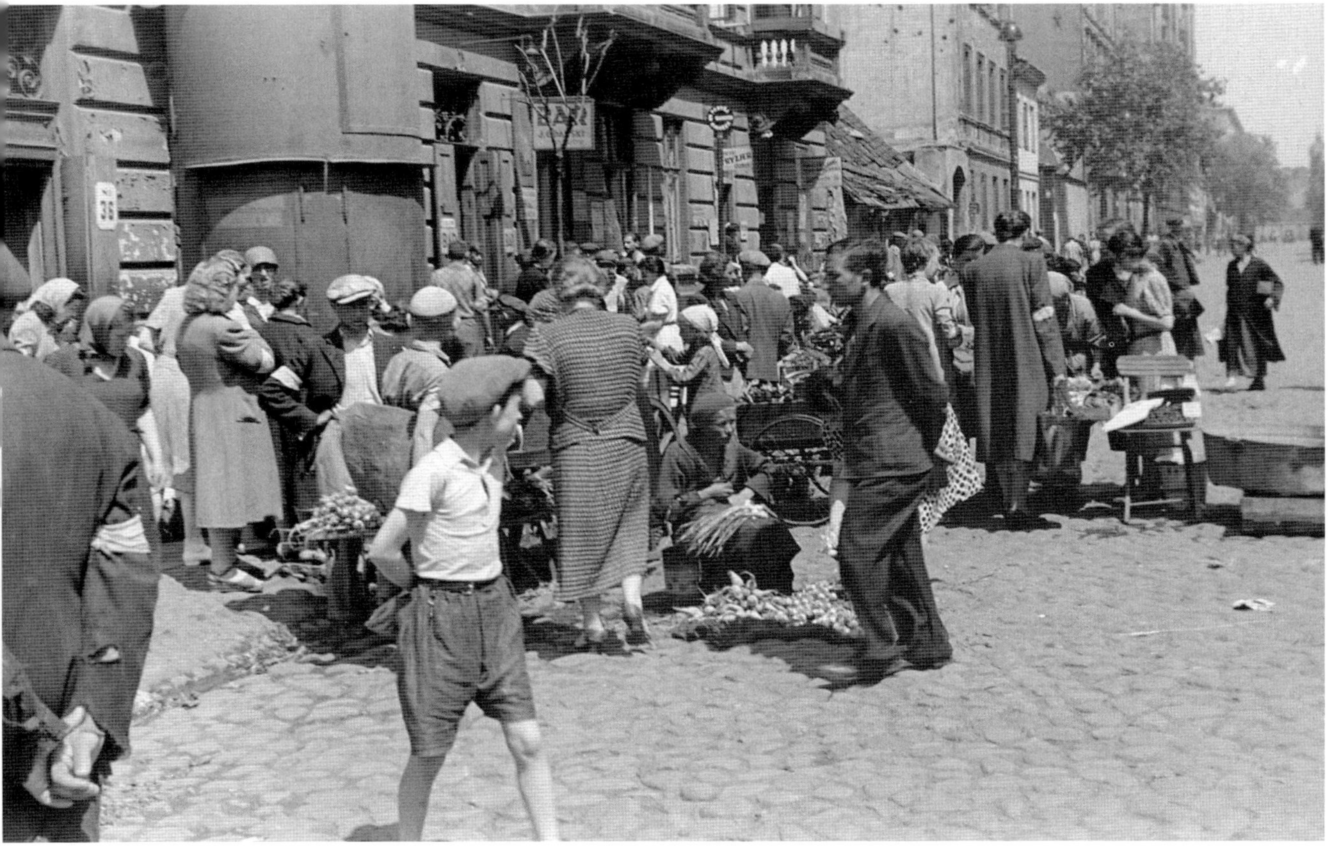
BAR
Nr
36

(**Above**) Jews converse on a street in the Warsaw ghetto. Some 100,000 inhabitants of the ghetto died of hunger or disease before the liquidation actions began. (*USHMM: Rafael Scharf*)

(**Opposite**) The first two of four photographs taken with the Leica camera of Willy Georg of ghetto residents buying from street vendors at an open air market in the Warsaw ghetto. (*USHMM: Rafael Scharf*)

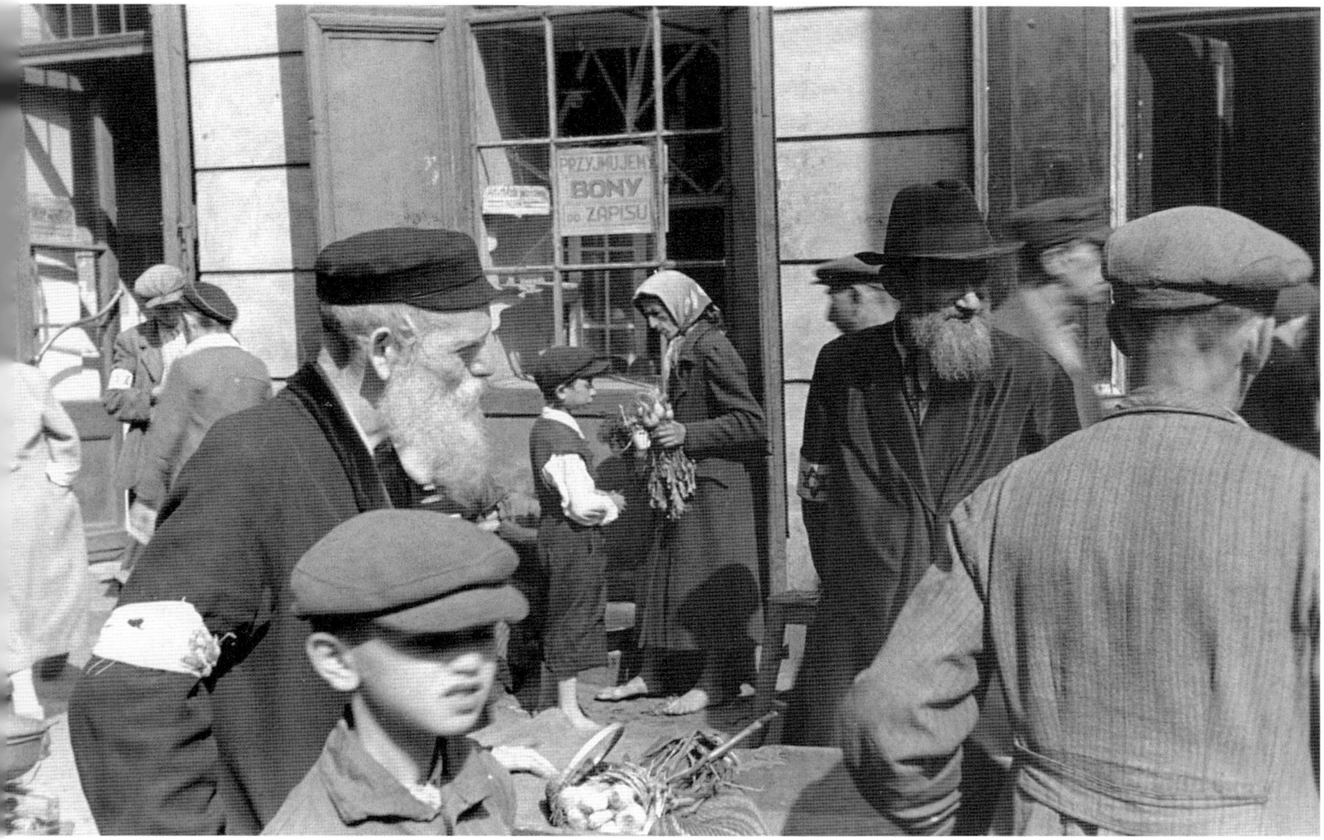
PRZYJMUJEMY
BONY
DO ZAPISU

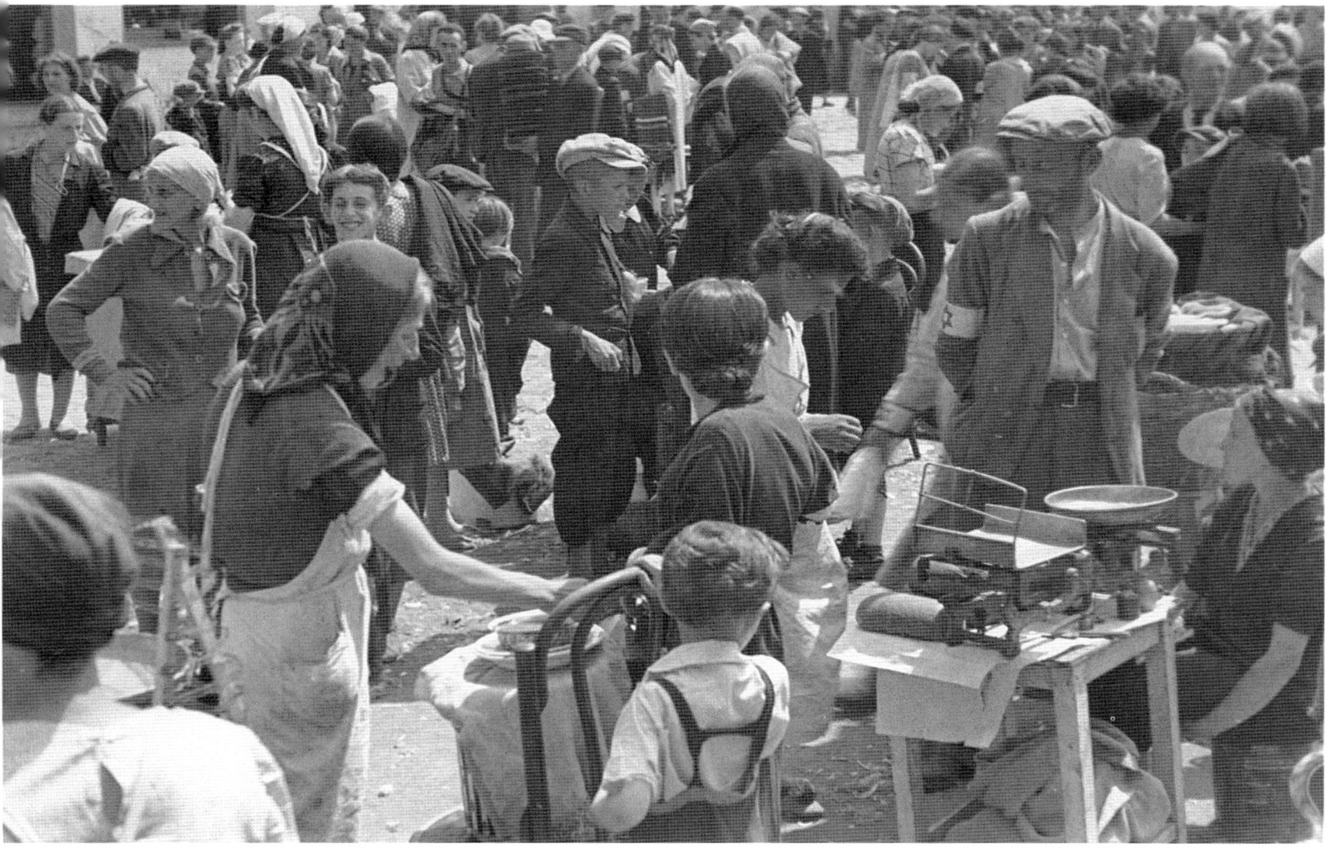

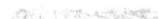

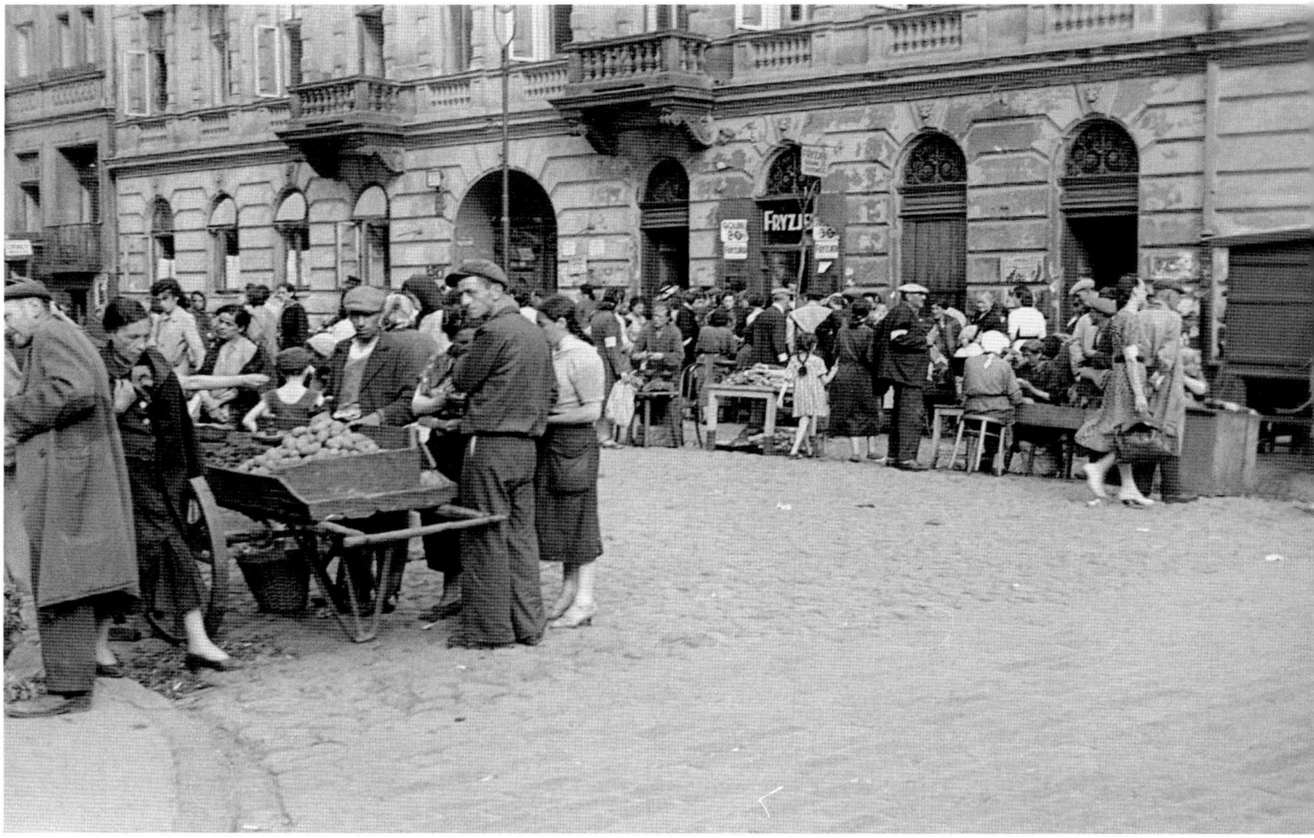

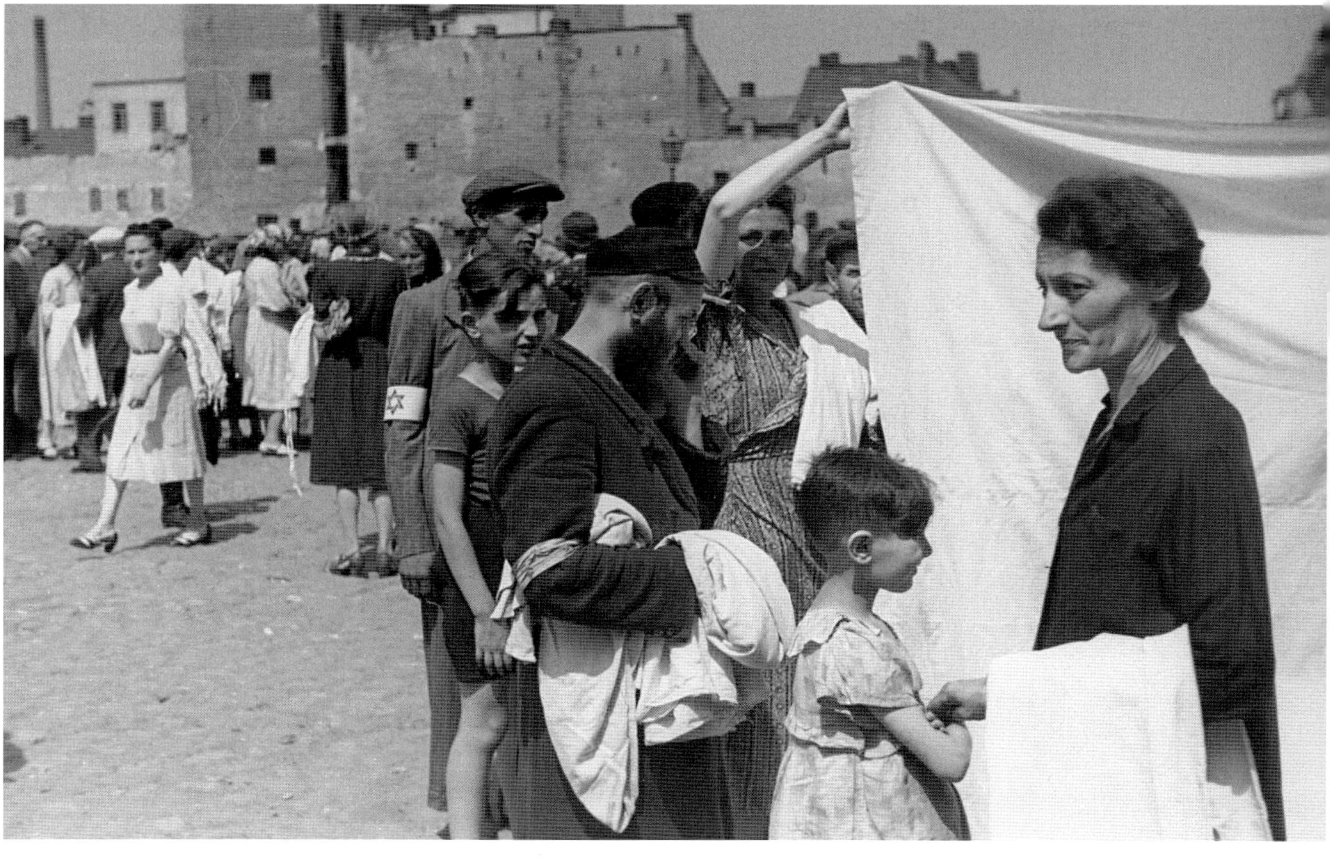

Another photograph by Willy Georg showing an elderly Jewish gentleman examining used clothing at an open air market in the Warsaw ghetto. *(USHMM: Rafael Scharf)*

(**Above**) Willy Georg captures a photograph showing a Jewish vendor offering odds and ends for sale at an open air market in the Warsaw ghetto. George shot four rolls of film during his time in the ghetto but had his camera confiscated while on the fifth. Fortunately the officer who confiscated his camera did not search him and he was able to get away with four rolls of film. It would not be until the late 1980s when George met Rafael Scharf, a researcher of Polish-Jewish Studies, that these images were revealed. (*USHMM: Rafael Scharf*)

(**Opposite, above**) Polish Jews wearing armbands walk along a street in an unidentified ghetto, probably early summer 1942. (*USHMM: Michael O'Hara*)

(**Opposite, below**) This photograph was taken in the summer of 1940 and shows a group of Jewish men marching off for a labour assignment in an unidentified Polish city. (*USHMM: Heide Brandes*)

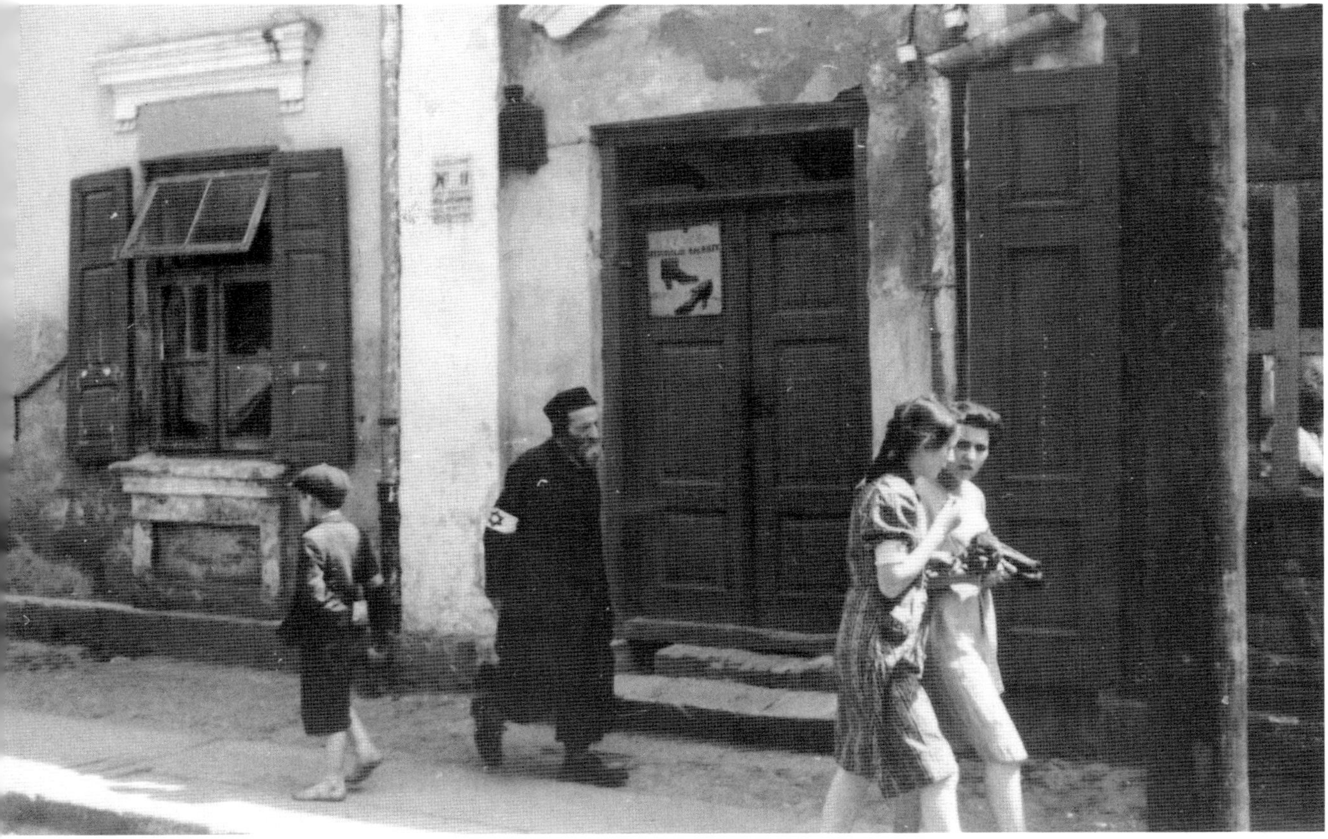

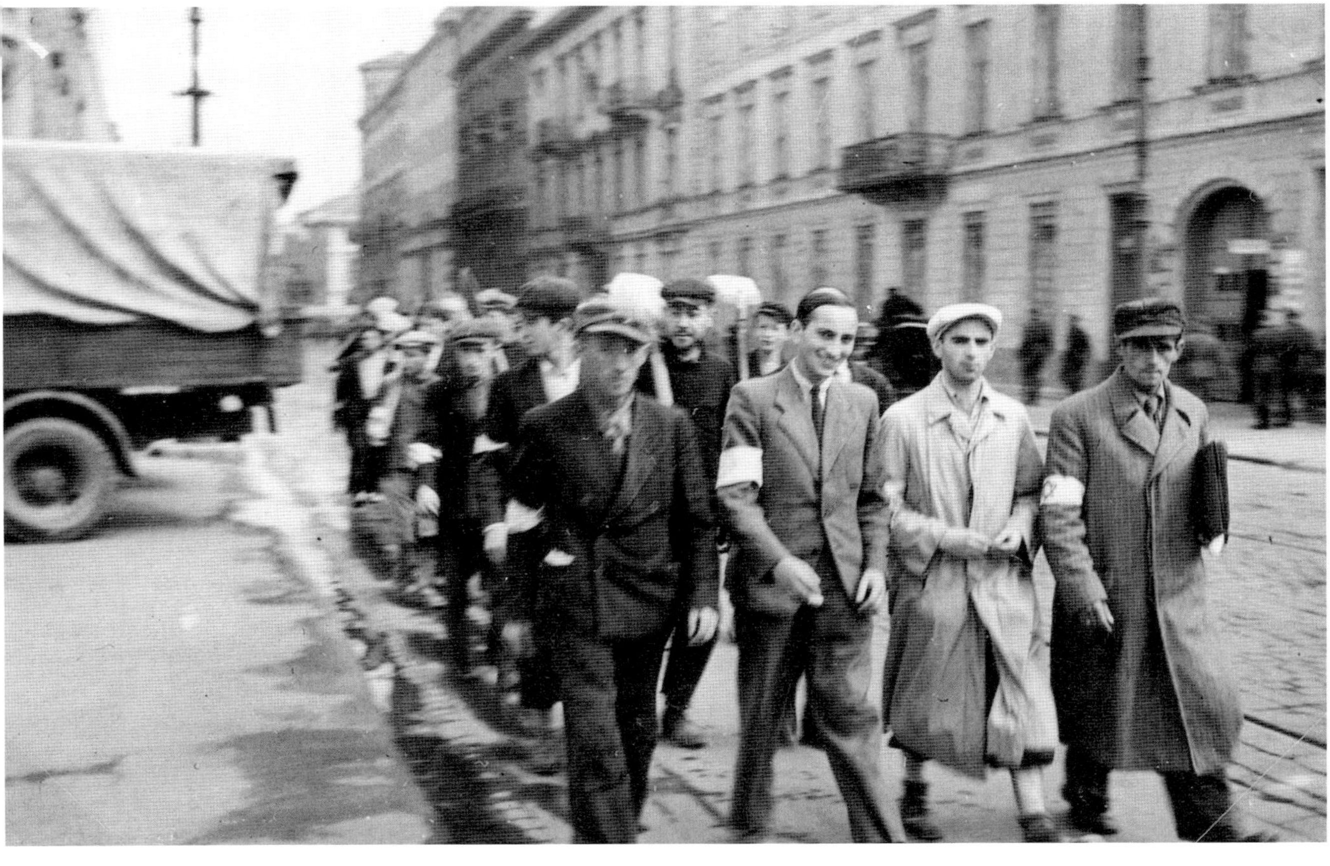

(**Above**) A photo taken in February 1941 showing ghetto inhabitants shovelling snow off a pavement. The original German caption read, 'The German police's main duty was to establish some sort of order especially since the Jews were not interested in cleanliness. When the German police arrived to the "control point" the Jews quickly began to sweep and shovel.' (*USHMM: Joseph Eaton*)

(**Opposite, above**) A group of Jewish forced labourers pose for the camera with shovels at the entrance to the Kolbuszowa Ghetto. In September 1941 the ghetto was established and some 2,500 Jewish people were incarcerated there. In September 1942 the ghetto was emptied and its entire population was moved to a ghetto in Rzeszow. (*USHMM: Norman Salsitz*)

(**Opposite, below**) Jewish women, with their children watching on, can be seen working on an agricultural plot in the Kovno ghetto. (*USHMM: George Kadish/Zvi Kadushin*)

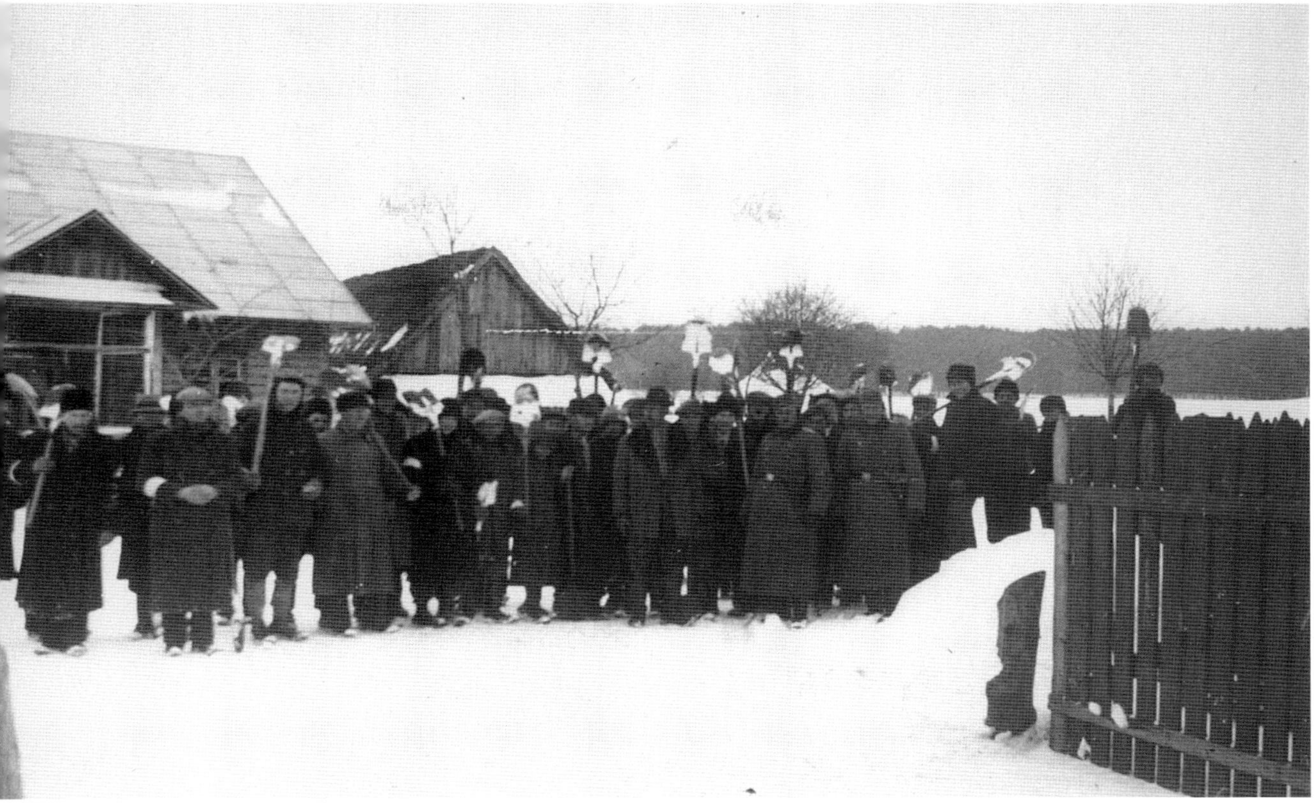

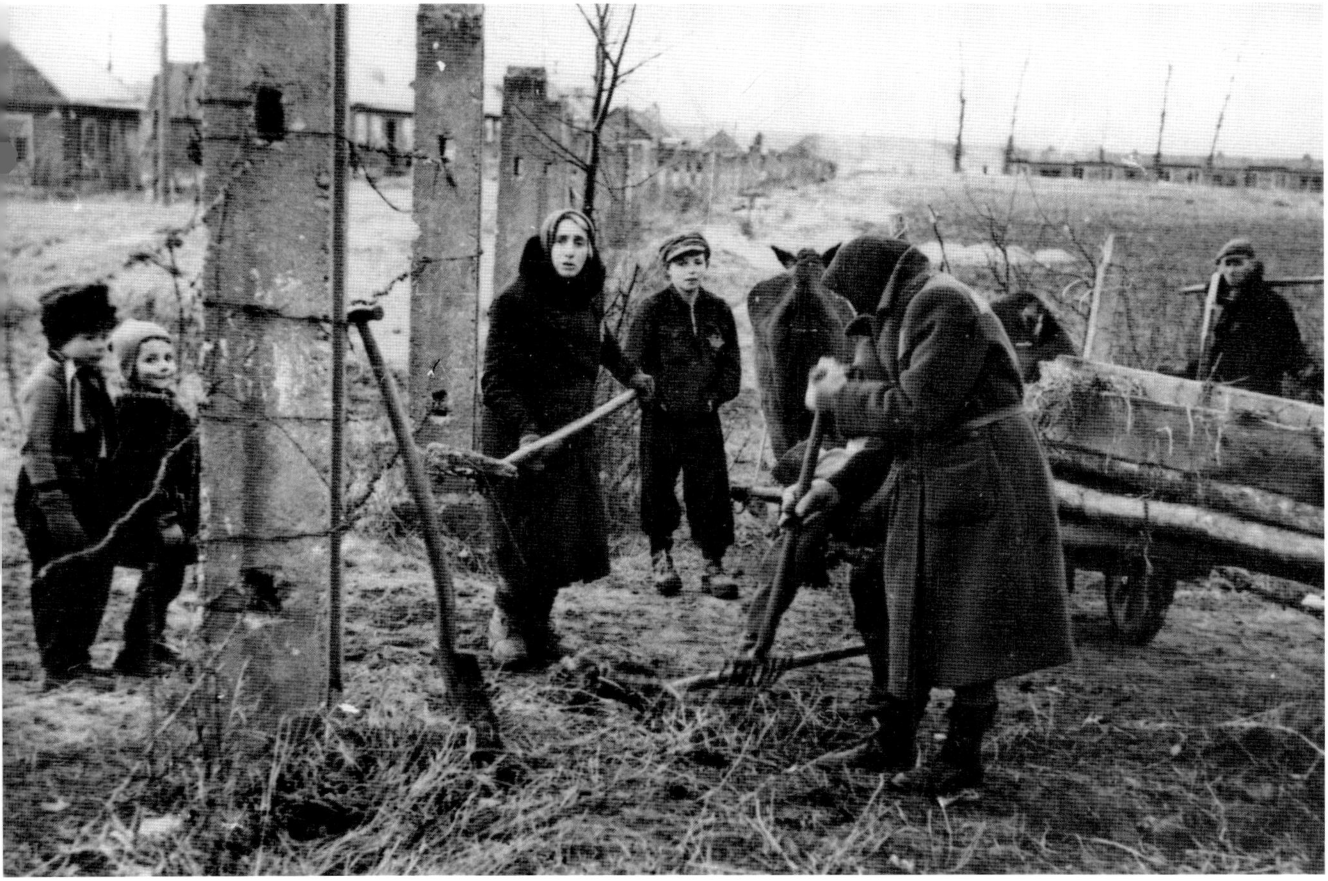

A elderly Polish Jew wearing a Jewish badge walks along a street in Dabrowa Gornicza. It appears that he has taken off his hat as the German photographer takes the photo. *(USHMM: Sima Malah)*

A photograph taken by Willy Georg showing a destitute child sleeping on the pavement in the Warsaw ghetto in the summer of 1941. *(USHMM: Rafael Scharf)*

A man lies dead on the pavement in front of a shop in the Warsaw ghetto. Starvation was rampant in the ghetto and diseases such as tuberculosis widespread. (*USHMM: Rafael Scharf*)

Two photographs showing Jewish woman lying dead on the street in the Warsaw ghetto. These photos were taken by Heinrich Joest, a German army sergeant stationed in Warsaw in 1941. On 19 September, his birthday, Joest took his Rolleiflex camera into the Warsaw ghetto because he wanted 'to see what went on behind the ghetto walls'. He shot 140 images there. It would not be until 1982 when he met Guenther Schwarberg, a reporter for *Stern* magazine, that his chilling images were published. *(USHMM: Guenther Schwarberg)*

45

Another photograph taken by Heinrich Joest. A destitute beggar on the street in the Warsaw ghetto. The original caption to the photograph read: 'I do not know if this man was truly laughing, or if he only grinned at me out of fear. He stank dreadfully of rotting flesh.' *(USHMM: Guenther Schwarberg)*

A Heinrich Joest image showing a destitute woman on the street in the Warsaw ghetto. Joest's caption reads: 'I believe that this woman was a black-marketeer offering something or other for sale. She fearfully hid the pot in front of me and was thoroughly afraid around the police.' (USHMM: Guenther Schwarberg)

A Heinrich Joest photo showing a destitute mother holding her child begging on a street in the Warsaw ghetto. Joest's caption reads, 'With a gesture of her bandaged hand this woman wanted to show me that her child had nothing to eat. She wore a headscarf wrapped in a blanket but had no shoes.' (*USHMM: Guenther Schwarberg*)

Heinrich Joest shot this photograph showing vendors at an open air market in the Warsaw ghetto. His original caption reads, 'They wanted to sell underwear, aprons, purses, slips [for dresses], and towels. But who bought these things?' (*USHMM: Guenther Schwarberg*)

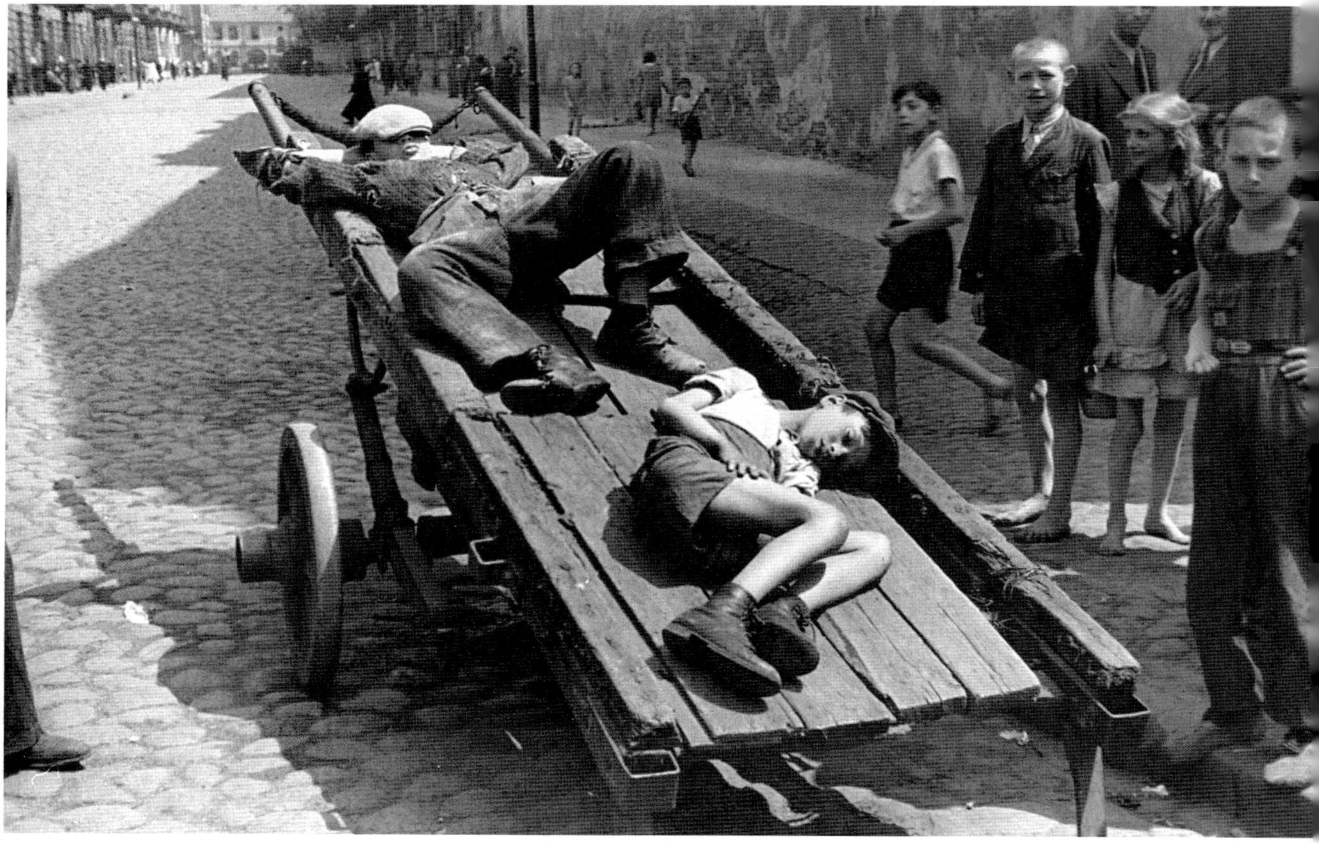

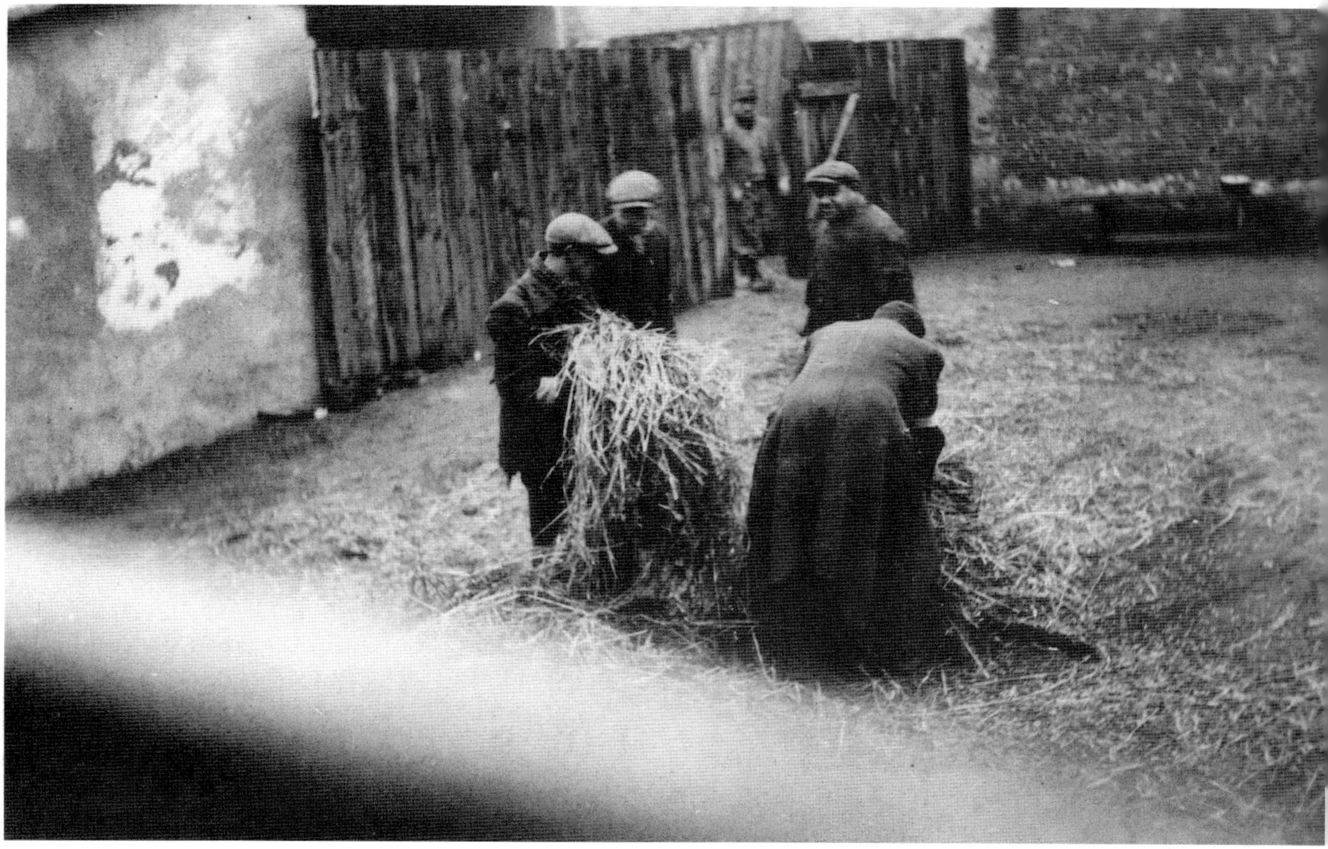

(**Opposite, above**) A Willy Georg photograph showing two destitute boys sleeping on a cart parked on a street in the Warsaw ghetto. (*USHMM: Rafael Scharf*)

(**Opposite, below**) Jews gather straw in the Zawiercie ghetto. In September 1941 the ghetto was created and contained about 5,500 Jews by the end of the year. In the summer of 1942 part of the ghetto was liquidated with about 2,000 inhabitants being sent to Auschwitz. It was fully liquidated in August 1943. (*USHMM*)

(**Above**) A photograph of a burial procession in the Warsaw ghetto cemetery taken by Heinrich Joest. His original caption reads, 'This was a "better" sort of funeral. The corpse was not put on a car but was carried wrapped in a shroud. A small procession of relatives followed behind. Evidently a well-do-do family – up to that point.' (*USHMM: Guenther Schwarberg*)

(**Above**) Heinrich Joest takes a photo of a group of destitute boys on a curb in the Warsaw ghetto. His original caption reads, 'It was striking to me how many youngsters did not wear shoes. It was already cold on this day. In the background of my photo I discovered later this Wehrmacht sergeant with his companion, a soldier. I thought to myself that he was going shopping in the ghetto, perhaps for jewellery.' *(USHMM: Guenther Schwarberg)*

(**Opposite**) Two photographs of Polish Jews wearing armbands on a busy street in an unidentified ghetto. *(USHMM: Michael O'Hara)*

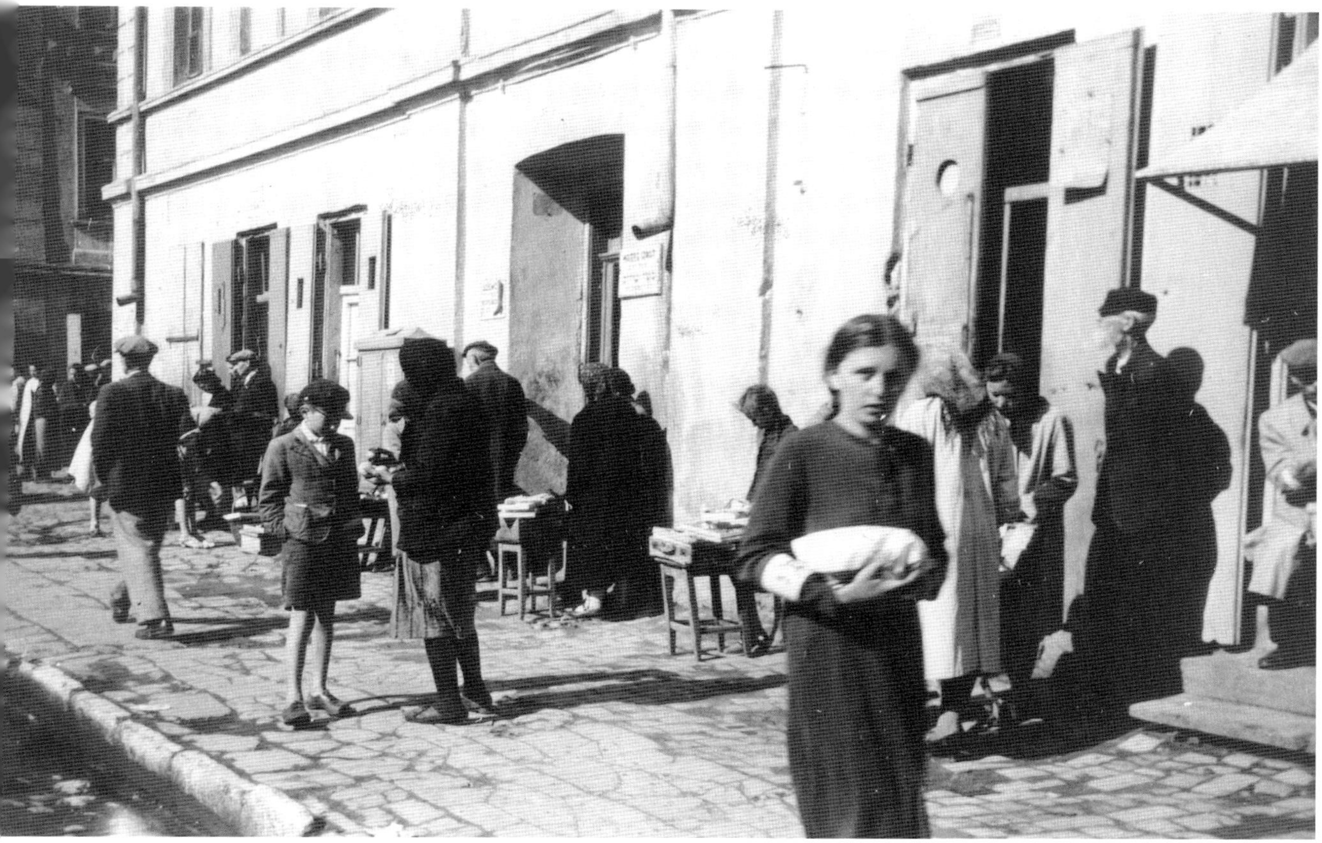

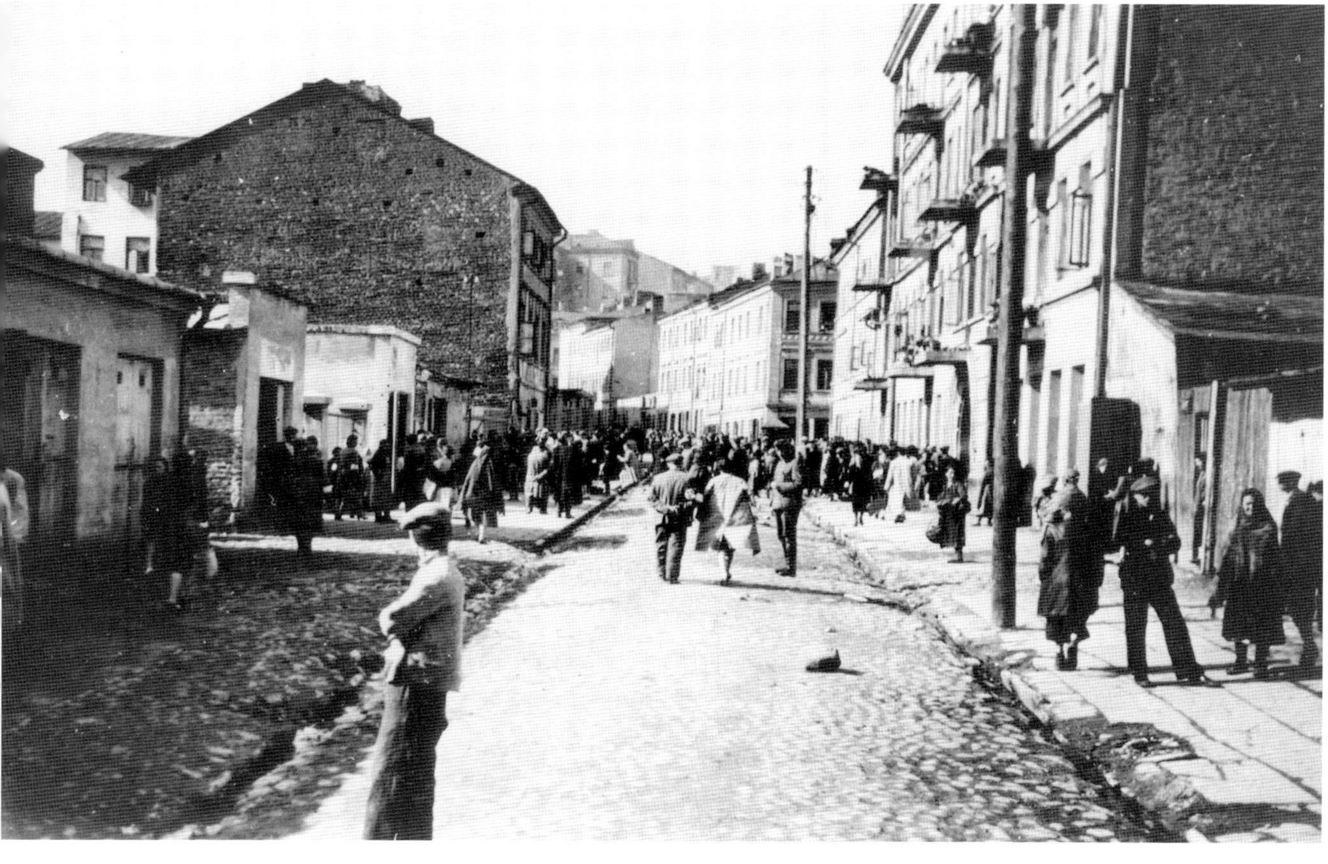

Chapter Three

Liquidation of the Ghettos

Initially the German authorities had no clear-cut plan how to deal with what they referred to as the 'Jewish issue', other than containing them throughout a vast ghetto system. However, at the Wannsee conference of January 1942, which was a meeting of senior Nazi officials and SS leaders, the 'final solution of the Jewish question' was decided upon. The plan was to deport all Jews to occupied Poland and murder them. The Jews in the General Government would be dealt with first.

It was suggested that a series of extermination camps was to be constructed in Poland, to kill Jews quickly and effectively. The codename given for the systematic annihilation of the Polish Jews in the General Government was Operation Reinhard.

There were to be three main camps used for the operation: Bełżec, Treblinka, and Sobibor. But the German authorities were under no illusion of the mammoth task ahead, and more would be needed.

During 1942 the liquidation of the ghettos began in earnest across the General Government. The German Reserve Police Battalion, together with members of the Jewish Police, the Sonderdienst battalion of Ukrainian Trawniki, supported by regular SS soldiers, were ordered to march into the ghettos and round up the Jews. (The Trawniki were Central and Eastern European collaborators recruited from Nazi PoW camps set up for Soviet Red Army soldiers captured in the border regions during the invasion of Russia.)

The Jews were either marched out of the ghetto or loaded on waiting trucks, then they were either transported directly to the camps or would board railway cattle or freight cars to their destination. The liquidation of the ghettos was often violent: the guards would beat and kill Jews in the streets.

The Częstochowa Ghetto, for instance, saw most of its 40,000 inhabitants boarded onto trains under the guise of resettlement, sent directly to Treblinka and murdered. From Miedzyrzec over 10,000 were rounded up by German Order Police battalions and deported to Treblinka. In the Minsk ghetto some 5,000 were forced out of their squalid living places onto freight trains bound for Treblinka.

In some of the ghettos, plans were made to murder the inhabitants *in situ*. Thousands were killed like this. Around 4,500 from the Izbica Ghetto were marched out of their ghetto and killed in mass pits. The Lida Ghetto saw nearly 6,000 forced out of their ghetto and taken to a nearby military firing range where they were shot in grave pits. In the summer of 1942, the liquidation of the Nowogródek ghetto began with the murdering of the *Judenräte*, either by being shot or hung. This was followed with about 1,200 Jews being forced out of the town and marched to the Kurpiasz Forest where they were all shot in hastily prepared pits. On 6 August 1942 between 2,000 and 3,000 Jews were executed in mass graves in the Jewish cemetery on the southern outskirts of Zdzięcioł.

The liquidation process was undertaken in phases. At the Końskowola ghetto, most of the inhabitants were rounded up in the summer of 1942 and transported to the Sobibor extermination camp, but it was not until October 1942 that the last of the ghetto would be liquidated. The final 800 to 1,000, many of them women and children, were taken to a nearby forest and massacred by Reserve Police Battalion 101. At the Buczacz ghetto in the summer of 1942 some 4,500 Jews were either murdered or transported to Bełżec. However, it would not be until early April 1943 that more than 2,000 Jews regarded as 'unskilled labour' were removed from the ghetto and murdered in pits near Fedor Hill. Shortly after that, more inmates of the ghetto were removed and sent to the Podheitzka labour camp. In April and May 1943, an additional 3,000 Jews were murdered. By June 1943, the last of the ghetto was liquidated with the remaining Jews deported or shot. In the Kraków ghetto, due to its size, the liquidation was done in phases. The first transport consisted of 7,000, the second 4,000, all deported to Bełżec in the summer of 1942. It was not until March 1943 that the final liquidation was carried out. Those deemed unfit for labour, around 2,000, were rounded up and either murdered in the streets of the ghetto or transported to Auschwitz. The 8,000 that were left were transported and forced to work in the Płaszów labour camp.

The clearing of the Warsaw ghetto (the largest ghetto in occupied Europe with some 460,000 Jews contained within its walls) was an immense undertaking. The responsibility for the shipments from Warsaw in liaison with the railway authorities of the *Ostbahn* was put in the hands of SS-Hauptsturmführer Hermann Höfle. The first phase of the operation was set in motion on 22 July 1942 – the Treblinka death camp railway station received a telegram saying that cattle trains would start travelling between Warsaw and Treblinka. It confirmed that the trains would have sixty closed cars each and that they would be transporting deportees from the Warsaw ghetto. At Treblinka camp they would be unloaded and then sent back empty. All the inhabitants from the ghetto were destined for the new death camp, code-named TII.

Höfle issued the following order to the Jewish Council in Warsaw:

> The Jewish Council is hereby informed of the following:
> 1. All Jewish persons irrespective of age or sex who live in Warsaw will be resettled in the east.

2. The following are excluded from the resettlement:
   (a) All Jewish persons who are employed by the German authorities or by German agencies and can provide proof of it.
   (b) All Jewish persons who belong to the Jewish Council and are employees of the Jewish Council.
   (c) All Jewish persons who are employed by German firms and can provide proof of it.
   (d) All Jews capable of work who have not hitherto been employed. They are to be placed in barracks in the ghetto.
   (e) All Jewish persons who are members of the personnel of the Jewish hospitals. Similarly, the members of the Jewish disinfection troops.
   (f) All Jewish persons who belong to the Jewish police force.
   (g) All Jewish persons who are close relatives of the persons referred to in (a)–(f). Such relatives are restricted to wives and children.
   (h) All Jewish persons who on the first day of the resettlement are in one of the Jewish hospitals and are not capable of being released. The fitness for release will be decided by a doctor to be designated by the Jewish Council.
2. Every Jewish person being resettled may take 15kg of his property as personal luggage. All valuables may be taken: gold, jewellery, cash etc. Food for three days should be taken.
4. The resettlement begins on 22 July 1942 at 11 o'clock.

II. The Jewish Council is responsible for providing the daily quota of Jews for transportation. To carry out this task the Jewish council will use the Jewish police force (100 men). The Jewish Council will ensure that every day from 22 July onwards, by 16.00 at the latest, 6,000 Jews will be assembled directly on the loading platform near the transfer office. To start with, the Jewish Council may take the quotas of Jews from the whole population. Later, the Jewish Council will receive special instructions according to which particular streets and blocks of flats are to be cleared.

VIII. Punishments:
(a) Any Jewish person who leaves the ghetto at the start of the resettlement without belonging to the categories of persons outlined in 2(a) and (c), and in so far as they were not hitherto entitled to do so, will be shot.
(b) Any Jewish person who undertakes an act which is calculated to evade or disturb the resettlement measures will be shot.
(c) Any Jewish person who assists in an act calculated to evade or disturb the resettlement measures will be shot.

(d) All Jews who, on completion of the resettlement are encountered in Warsaw and do not belong to the categories referred to in 2(a)-(h), will be shot.

The Jewish council is hereby informed that, in the event that the orders and instructions are not carried out 100%, an appropriate number of the hostages who have been taken in the meantime will be shot.

The liquidation of the Warsaw ghetto was a massive deportation action in which 265,000 ghetto residents were sent to the Treblinka extermination camp and some 20,000 to labour camps. This process took twelve weeks to achieve and it soon became apparent to the Jews left inside the ghetto that these were deportations to death camps. What followed was a ghetto uprising in April 1943.

Uprisings had not been uncommon during the liquidation process of the ghettos, and the German authorities fought back, with harsh consequences for both perpetrators and the innocent. However the most famous was that in the Warsaw ghetto. This uprising raged for three and a half weeks and was contested fiercely by 2,000 Waffen-SS troops. It was a bloodbath on both sides and the ghetto was razed to the ground.

A portrait photo of Reinhard Heydrich, the architect for the murder of the Polish Jews. At the Wannsee conference in January 1942, Heydrich chaired a meeting to discuss 'the final solution of the Jewish question'.

Reichsführer-SS Heinrich Himmler reviews a unit of SS-police in Kraków in the company of Friedrich-Wilhelm Krueger on 13 March 1942. Later that evening, Himmler met with General Governor Hans Frank. At that meeting, Himmler communicated the message that by the end of 1942 half of all the Jews in the General Government would be murdered. *(USHMM: James Blevins)*

Two photographs show German soldiers overseeing Jews from the Zyrardow ghetto boarding a deportation train. (*USHMM: Instytut Pamięci Narodowej*)

Three elderly Jews walk arm-in-arm through the streets of Kraków during the final liquidation of the ghetto in March 1943. *(USHMM: Instytut Pamieci Narodowej)*

A column of Jews march with bundles down a main street in Kraków during the liquidation of the ghetto. SS guards oversee the deportation. *(USHMM: Instytut Pamieci Narodowej)*

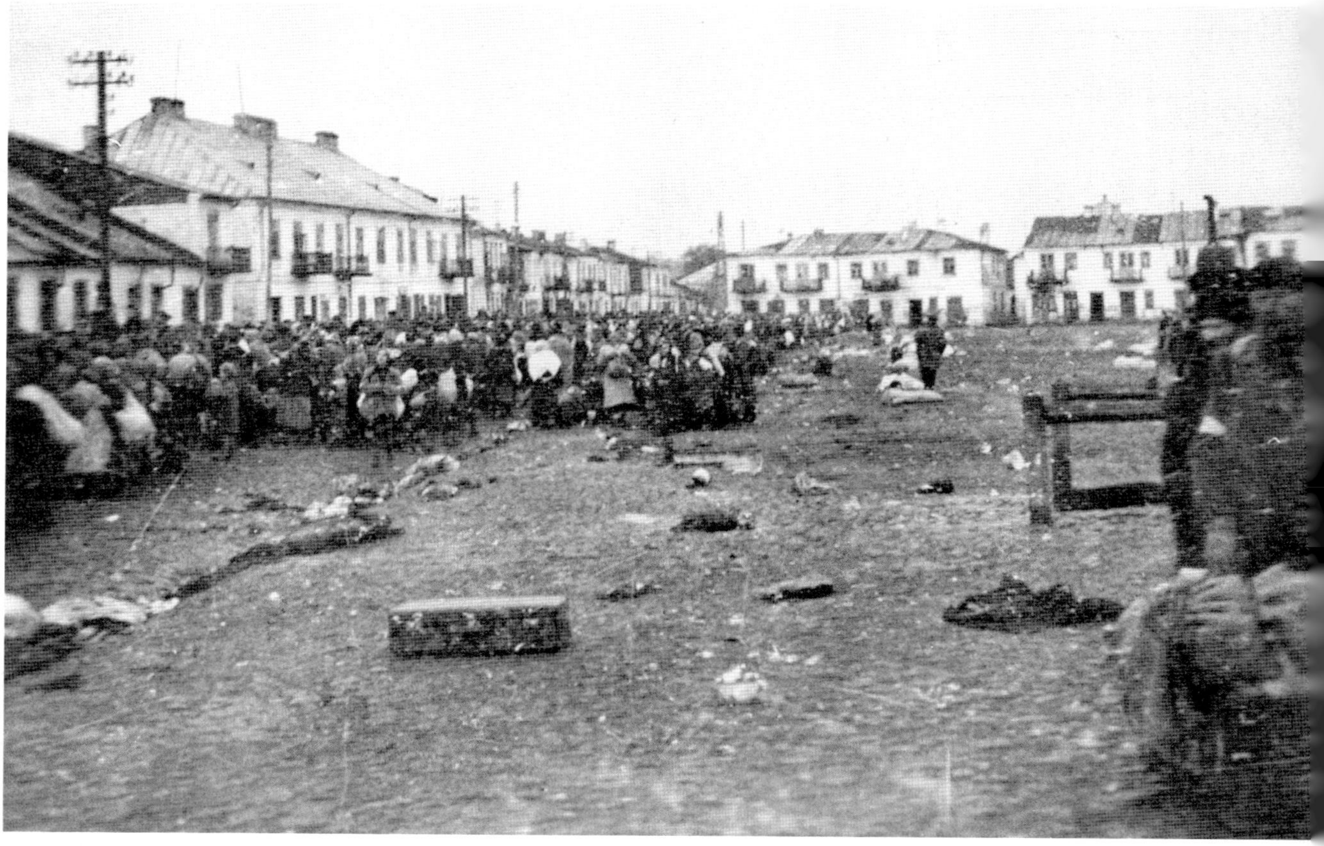

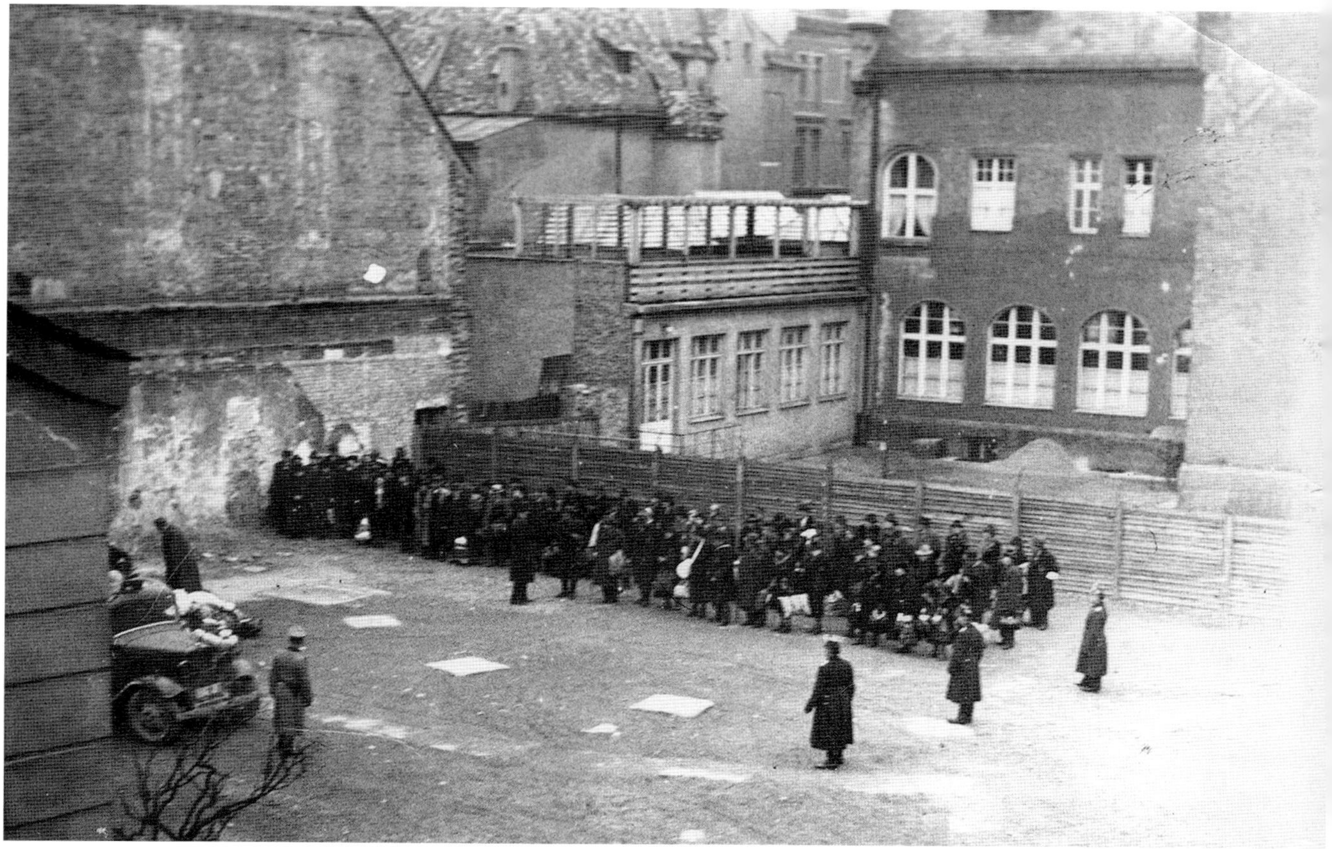

(**Opposite, above**) Jews are rounded up for deportation in the Wisznice ghetto. *(USHMM: Eliezer & Jenelly Rosenberg)*

(**Opposite, below**) German soldiers are seen rounding up Jews on Francuska Street in the Dombrowa ghetto. *(USHMM: Sidney Schlesinger)*

(**Above**) View of a major street in Kraków following the liquidation of the ghetto. Strewn across the street are bundles of possessions left behind by the Jews who were hurriedly removed from the ghetto in March 1943. *(USHMM: Instytut Pamieci Narodowej)*

(**Above**) Jews wearing circular badges walk through town during a deportation action from the Krzemieniec ghetto. During the liquidation of the ghetto on 22 July 1942, there was armed resistance by the Jews against the Germans. But the resistance was short-lived and the surviving inhabitants were rounded up and deported. Some 19,000 were killed in this action. (*USHMM: Instytut Pamieci Narodowej*)

(**Opposite, above**) German police round up Jews and load them onto trucks in the Ciechanow ghetto during the liquidation. (*USHMM: Instytut Pamieci Narodowej*)

(**Opposite, below**) Jews from the Ciechanow ghetto are marched out of town to a fortress to be contained there before the ghetto is liquidated. Most of the Jews in this photograph were eventually transported to the Red Forest north-east of the town and murdered by gunfire. (*USHMM: Instytut Pamieci Narodowej*)

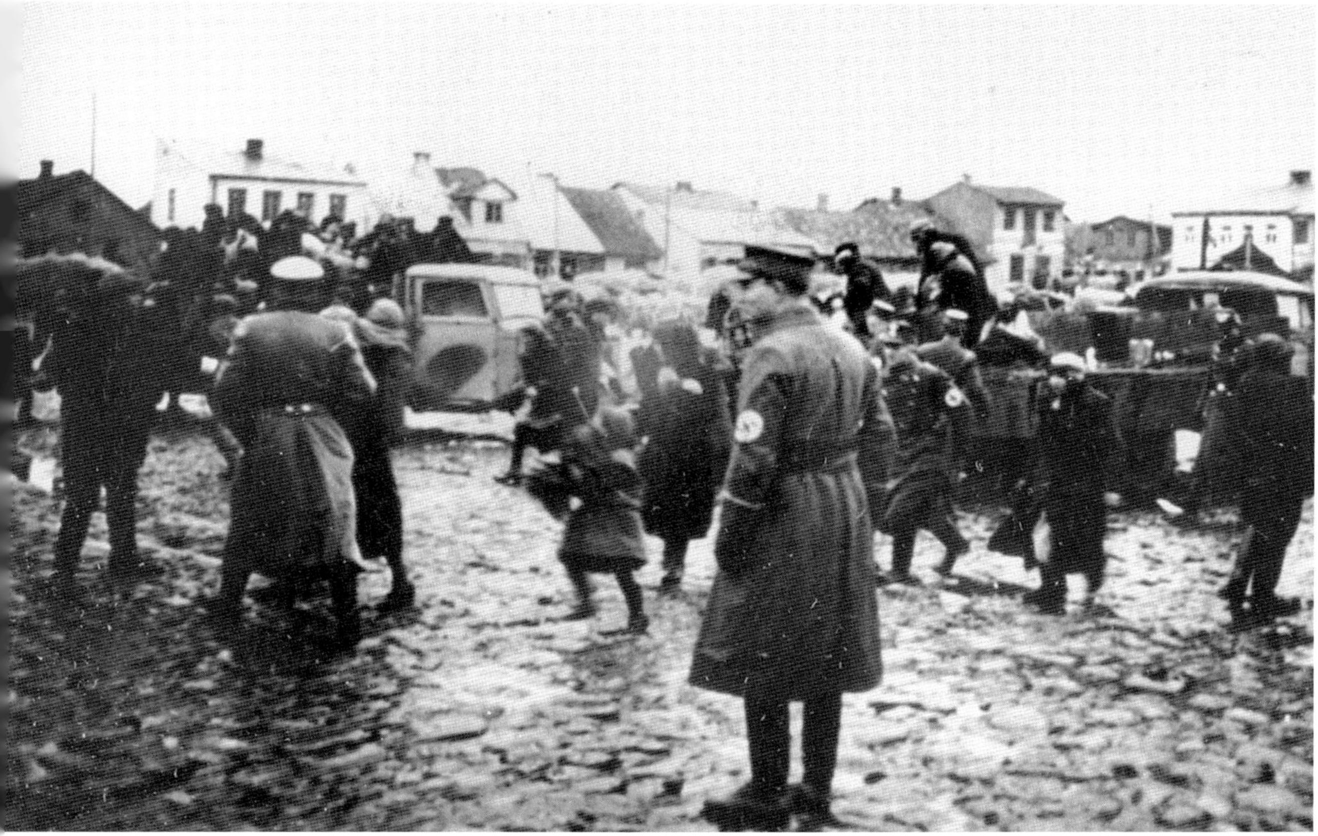

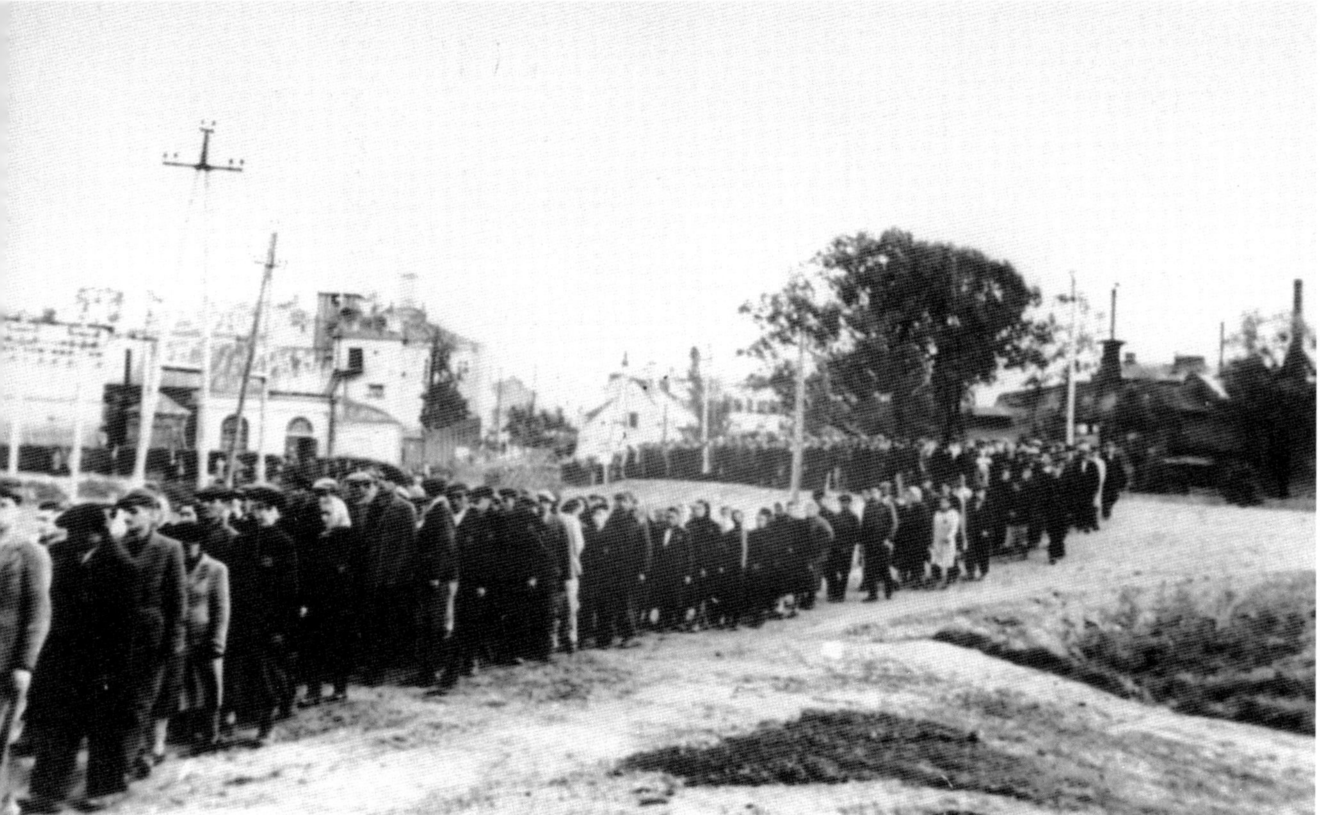

(**Above**) Jews from the Ciechanow ghetto are assembled in a fortress. During the war many Polish Jews and resistance fighters were executed by the Germans in the castle. (*USHMM: Instytut Pamieci Narodowej*)

(**Opposite, above**) A German policeman prepares to complete a mass execution of the remaining inhabitants of the Mizocz ghetto by shooting two Jewish children, who can still be seen sitting up looking very distressed. The Mizocz Ghetto had initially held some 1,700 Jews. On 13 October 1942, the eve of the ghetto's liquidation, some of the inhabitants rose up against the Germans and were defeated after a short battle. The remaining members of the community were transported from the ghetto to a ravine in the Sdolbunov, south of Rovno. At the edge of the ravine the Jews, mainly women and children, were ordered to undress, herded down the ravine, and then shot. (*USHMM: Instytut Pamieci Narodowej*)

(**Opposite, below**) A column of Jews marches through the streets of Kraków during the final liquidation of the ghetto. (*USHMM: Instytut Pamieci Narodowej*)

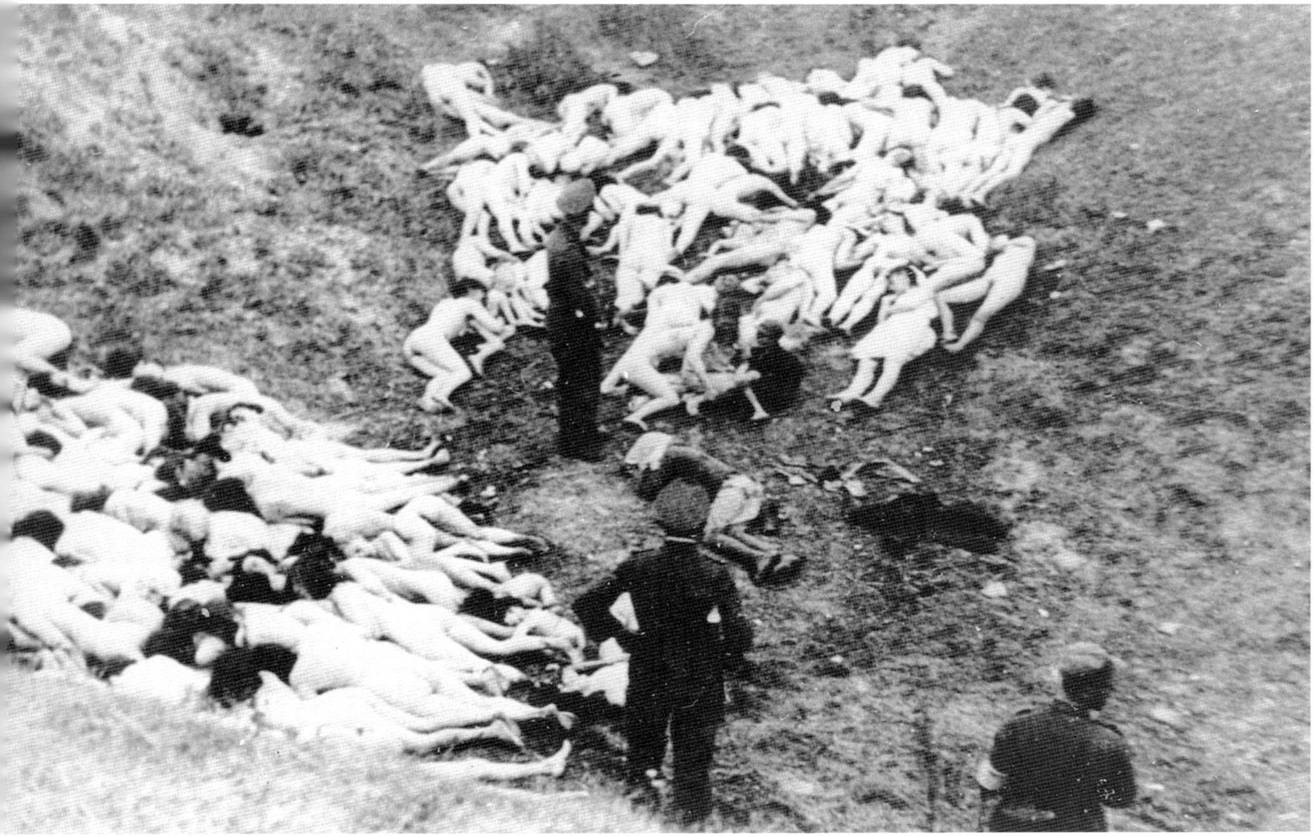

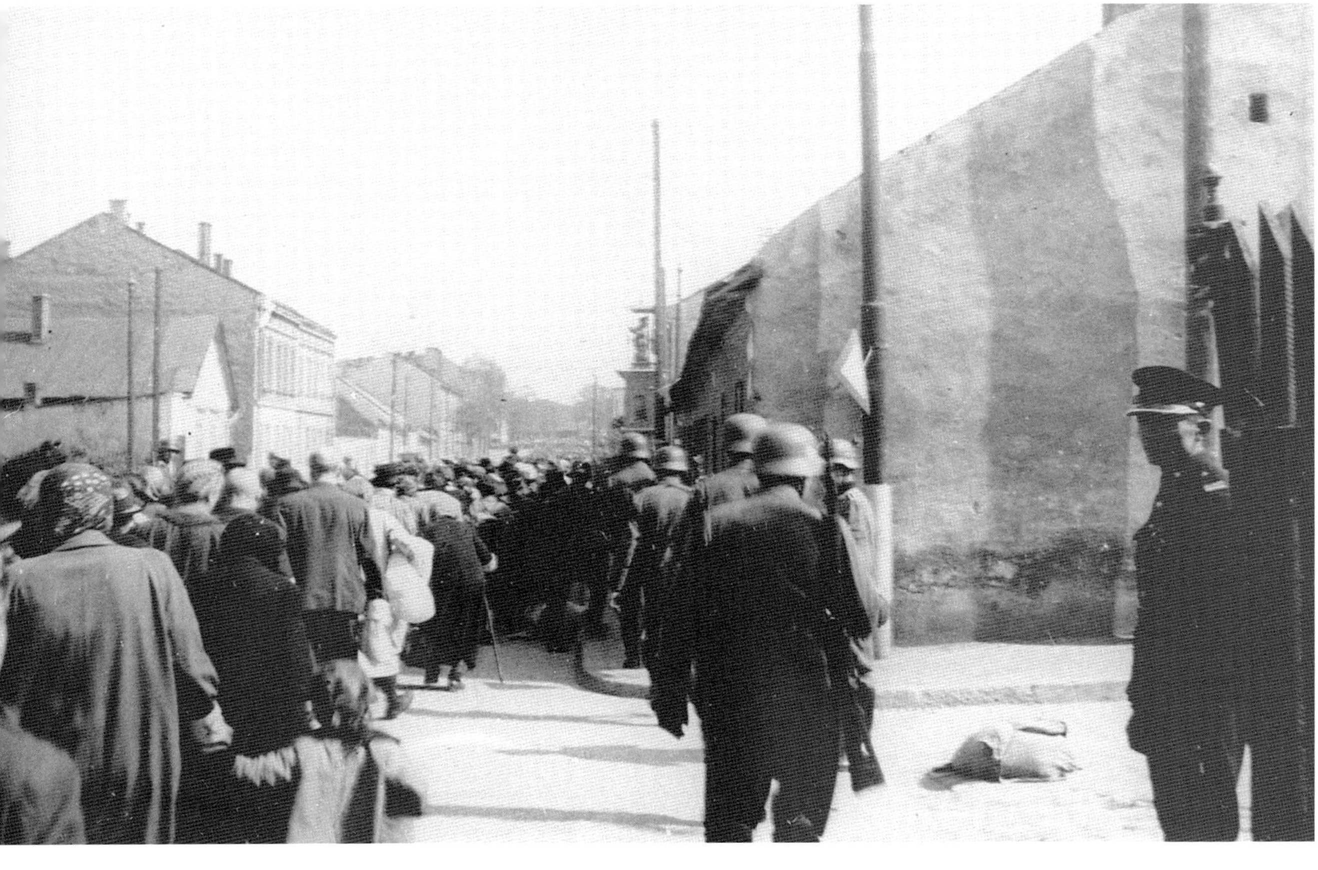

Deutsche
Reichsbahn
München
29486
G
29486

Deutsche
Reichsbahn
Karlsruhe
34 234
G

(**Opposite**) Two photographs showing SS soldiers supervising the boarding of Jews onto trains during a deportation action in the Kraków ghetto in March 1943. (*USHMM: Archiwum Dokumentacji Mechanicznej*)

(**Above**) Jews from the Łódź ghetto board deportation trains to the Chełmno death camp. Some 55,000 Jews were sent to Chełmno between January and May 1942. Four months later a further 15,000 were deported in a second phase of the liquidation of the ghetto. They were all sent directly to Chełmno. There were no further deportations to death camps from Łódź for the next one and a half years, but from 23 June to 15 July 1944 some 7,000 Jews were deported to Chełmno. Thereafter, all deportation trains were routed to Auschwitz. The transports to Auschwitz commenced on 7 August and continued until 30 August, by which time more than 74,000 Jews had been sent to their deaths there. After this final transport, 1,200 Jews remained in two assembly camps in Łódź. Roughly half of them were soon transferred to labour camps in Germany.

Four photographs showing Jews boarding a train during a deportation action in the Łódź ghetto. The original German caption reads: '*Judenaussiedlung* [resettlement of Jews], April 1942'. By this time some 34,000 Jews had been deported by rail like this and sent directly to the Chełmno death camp. Although the German authorities had told the Jews they would be resettled further east, it had already become common knowledge that the mass executions were taking place. Some parents fearing the inevitable committed collective suicide to avoid their children suffering at the hands of the Nazis. *(USHMM: Robert Abrams)*

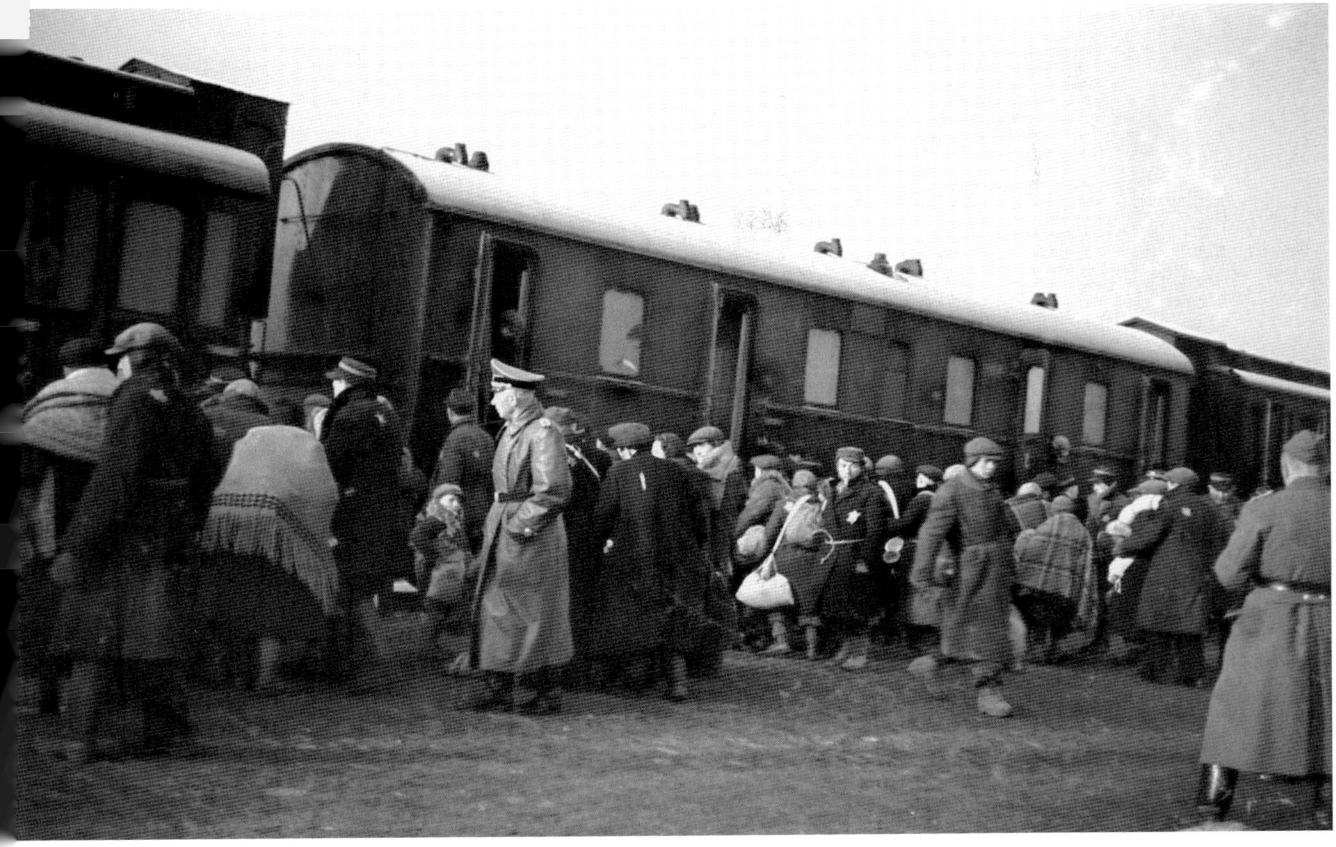

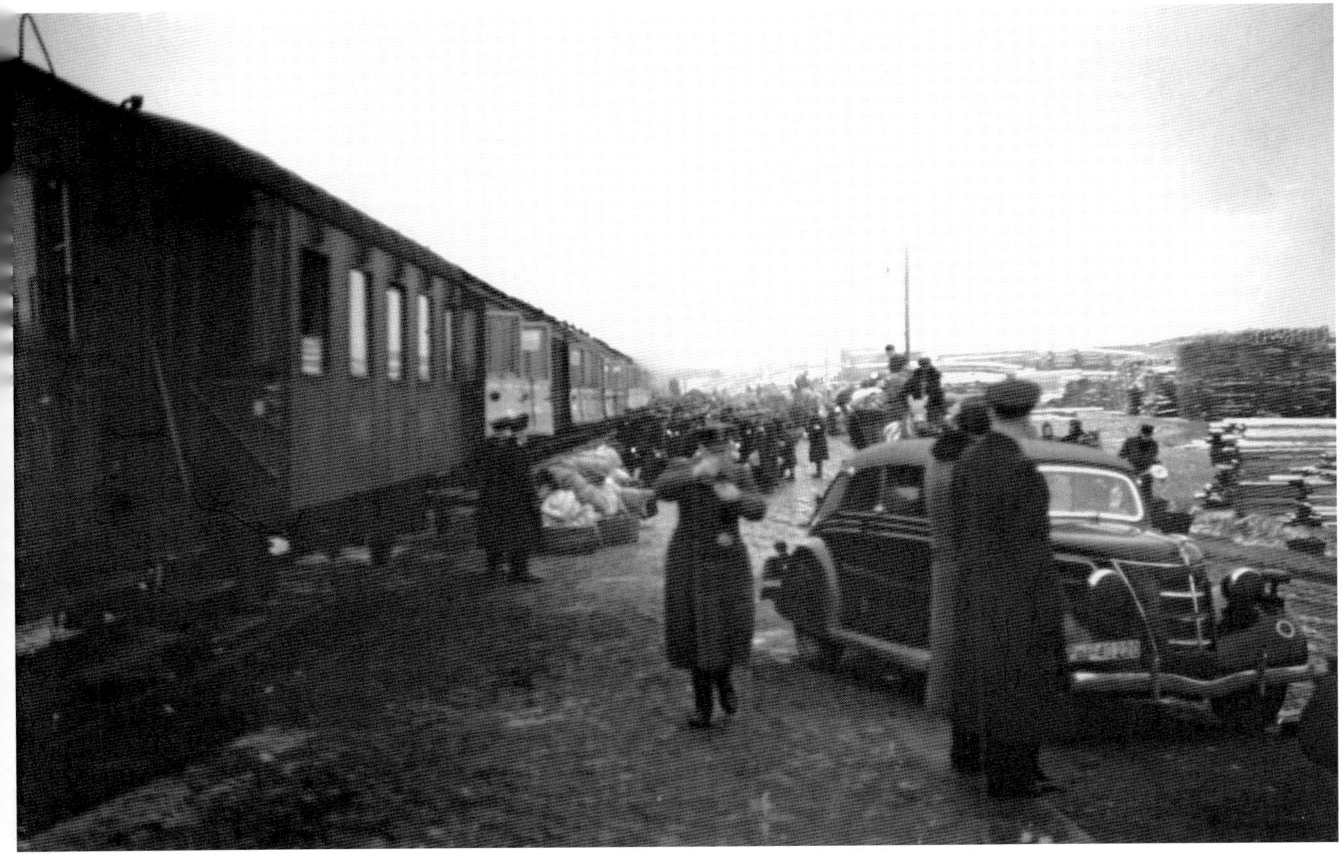

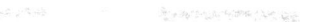

Jews from the Warsaw ghetto board a deportation train with the assistance of Jewish police. *(USHMM: Instytut Pamięci Narodowej)*

Chapter Four

The Warsaw Uprising 1943

The liquidation of the Jewish ghettos in Poland had a serious impact on the German war production effort there. The deportation of the Jews from the Warsaw ghetto to the Treblinka death camp for instance halved textile production. As a result, the German civilian and military authorities responsible for overseeing production in the occupied territories proposed that the Jews who were engaged in war production should not be murdered at quite such a rapid rate. Senior SS officials in the General Government had also become concerned, not least because they had employed Jewish labour for their own lucrative businesses.

In January 1943, the SS in the General Government proposed that all remaining fit or skilled Jews could be hired out to businesses for cash on a daily basis, returning to their living quarters at night.

What the German authorities did not realise, however, was that these fit and skilled workers were not so enthusiastic about being worked to exhaustion and eventually shipped off to a death camp and murdered. Inside the Warsaw ghetto, where more than 250,000 Jews had already been deported to their deaths, a large group began building bunkers and smuggling in weapons and explosives. The Jewish Combat Resistance group (ZOB) and the Jewish Military Unit (ZZW) were formed and began secretly training for combat.

On 18 January 1943 the Germans began their second liquidation phase of the Warsaw ghetto, and while Jewish families hid in their new bunkers and hideouts, the resistance groups began clashing with the German authorities. Losses among the resistance fighters were heavy and the Germans also took casualties. The fighting successfully reduced the number of Jews deported: only 5,000 were removed from the ghetto, instead of the intended 8,000.

The success of this uprising, however small it was, spurred on the resistance fighters, and now hundreds of people in the Warsaw ghetto were prepared to fight. Men, women and children, armed with various meagre weapons, Molotov cocktails, and a few other weapons that had been smuggled into the ghetto, were ready to protect themselves in a battle of honour of the Jewish people. Between February and March 1943, the resistance groups grew, in readiness for the final liquidation of the ghetto.

On 19 April, on the eve of Passover, police and SS auxiliary units, led by Ferdinand von Sammern-Frankenegg, entered the ghetto to finally liquidate it and deport all the Jews to Treblinka. Almost immediately these forces were ambushed by resistance fighters throwing Molotov cocktails and hand grenades and firing guns from their hideouts, the windows of buildings, and from the sewers. Fifty-nine police and SS troops were killed or injured.

Von Sammern-Frankenegg's failure to contain the revolt led to him being removed from his post as the SS and police commander of Warsaw. He was replaced by SS-Brigadeführer Jürgen Stroop.

Stroop sent in 2,000 well-armed troops including Waffen-SS and Panzergrenadier, as well as a strong contingent of Polish policemen. Also joining the task force was an anti-tank battery, a battalion of Ukrainian Trawniki men from the Trawniki training camp, Ukrainian, Lithuanian and Latvian auxiliary policemen known as Askaris (Latvian Arajs Commandos and Lithuanian Saugumas), and a technical emergency corps.

When Stroop's force marched into the ghetto, savage fighting immediately broke out. It took ten days for the units to gain the upper hand, but the fighting still raged. Although it became a disorganised defence, which collapsed in a number of areas, the survivors continued resisting. Women and children took cover in the sewage system and in the dugouts, remaining bunkers and hideouts among the burning ruins. The Germans used dogs to locate the hideouts and used smoke bombs to drive out the insurgents and terrified civilians. Sometimes they flooded the bunkers or destroyed them with high-explosives, or took armed units down into the sewers to shoot everyone they could find. Even after surrendering, there were some fanatical insurgents who had concealed hand grenades or small firearms on them.

The uprising finally ceased on 16 May 1943 with the Great Synagogue of Warsaw being destroyed by explosives, personally detonated by Stroop himself. Some 13,000 Jews were killed in the ghetto during the uprising. Of the remaining 50,000 residents, most were captured and marched out of the smouldering ruins of the ghetto destined for the Treblinka death camp.

When the first trainload arrived from Warsaw to Treblinka, the SS personnel noticed that the box cars were in terrible condition. According to one of the soldiers accompanying the train to the death camp some prisoners had frantically tried to escape by pulling apart the wooden flooring and other internal fixings.

When they were finally unloaded at the Treblinka, there was a sense of anxiety among the SS in the camp. The commandant had given his men strict instructions to move the Warsaw deportees through as quickly as possible to avoid panic and disorder. As they were unloaded under armed guard they were quickly escorted through to the camp square to be undressed. While they undressed there was an explosion, which wounded three prisoners and a few of the new arrivals. The SS men and the Ukrainian guards that had surrounded the square bolted for cover fearing there would be more explosions. After a few moments an alarm was raised and more guards came running to the square, and quickly sealed off the area. It soon became apparent that the explosion had been a hand grenade hidden in one the 'uprisers' pockets.

Once the confusion had settled the Ukrainian guards under the supervision of the SS herded the deportees together. Those lying injured on the ground from the hand grenade explosion were shot, the rest were led naked to their deaths. Many were kicked, punched and whipped as they were forced to run towards the gas chambers.

A long column of Jews who have been rounded up for deportation walk with their luggage along a street in the Warsaw ghetto. (*USHMM: Louis Gonda*)

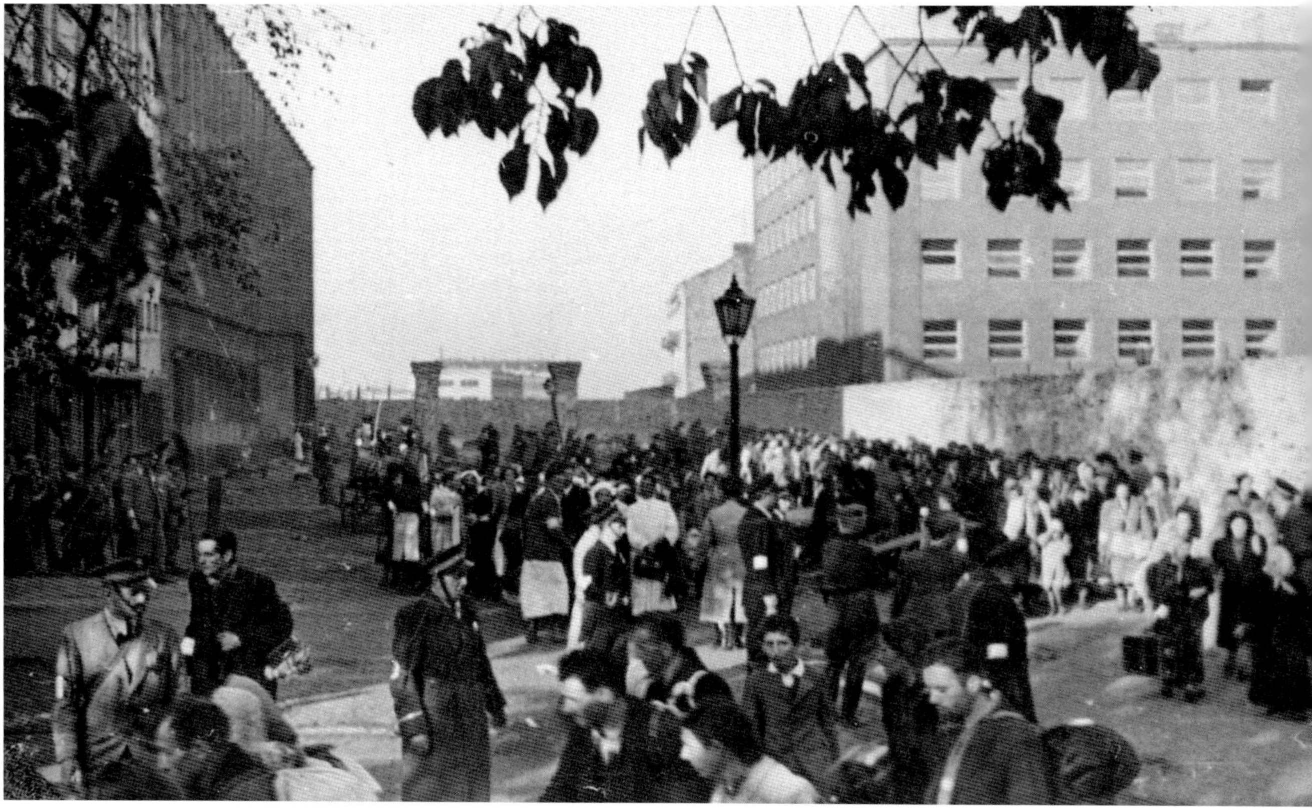

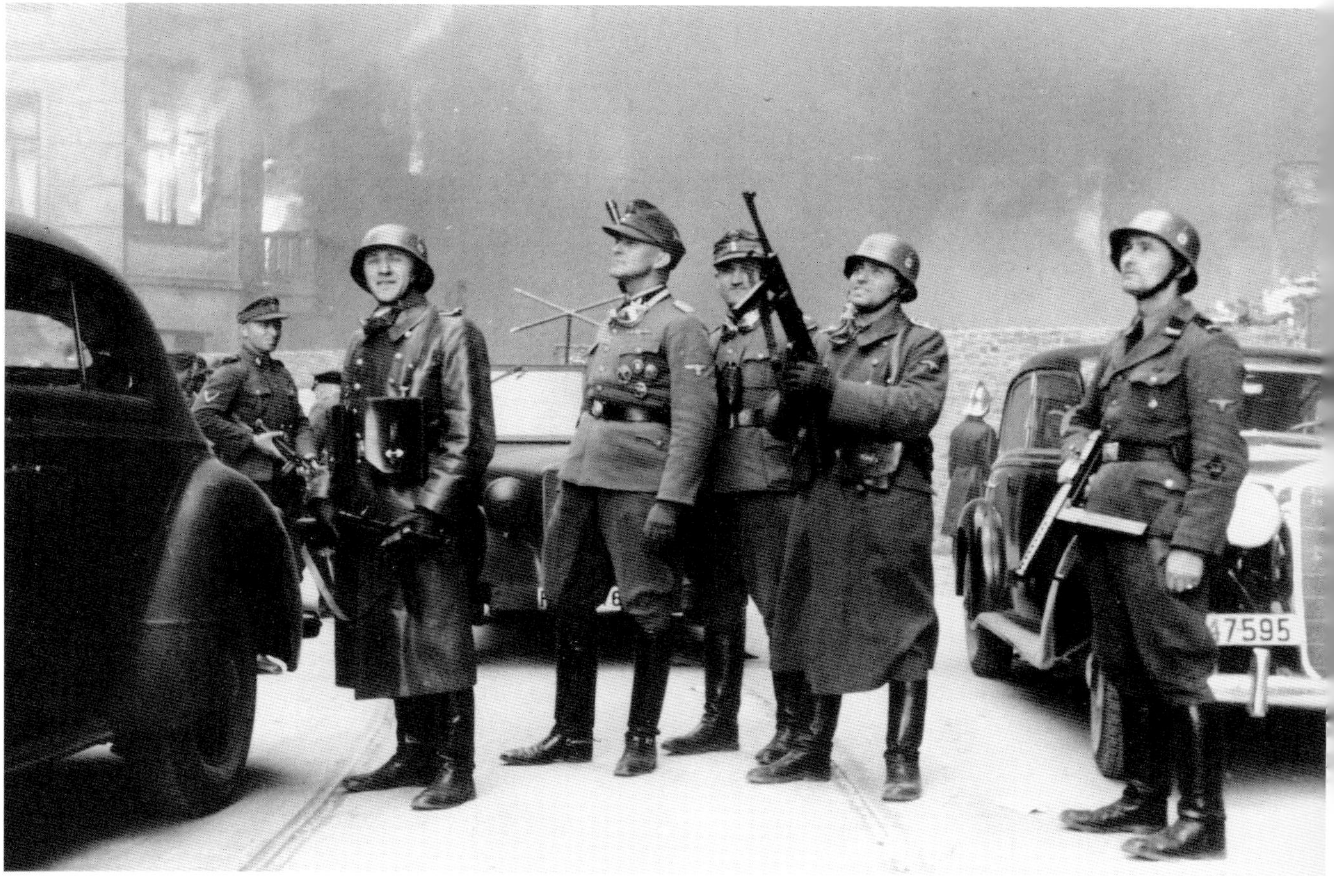
47595

(**Opposite, above**) A photograph showing Jews assembled for deportation at the Umschlagplatz in the Warsaw ghetto. The process of this liquidation comprised of Jews being either marched out of the ghetto or loaded onto waiting trucks and transported directly to the camps, or would have to board railway cattle or freight cars to their destination. (*USHMM: Instytut Pamieci Narodowej and Yad Vashem*)

(**Opposite, below**) Surrounded by heavily armed SS and SD guards, SS Major General Juergen Stroop (centre), watches housing blocks burn during the suppression of the Warsaw ghetto uprising. (*USHMM: National Archives*)

(**Above**) German police and an SS soldier man a machine gun during the suppression of the Warsaw ghetto uprising. The original German caption reads: 'Securing a street.' (*USHMM: National Archives*)

SS troops walk past a block of burning housing during the suppression of the Warsaw ghetto uprising. The original German caption reads: 'An assault squad.' (USHMM: National Archives)

SS soldiers take a break to eat during the suppression of the Warsaw ghetto uprising. (USHMM: Louis Gonda)

Polish fire fighters and SS officers in the Warsaw ghetto during the suppression of the uprising. The original Polish caption reads, 'The Germans set fire to the buildings evacuated by the Jews. From a balcony on the top floor a family of five or six people jumped to their deaths. They didn't leave earlier as ordered and then they couldn't run away. We didn't help them even though technically we could have.' *(USHMM: Howard Kaplan)*

SS and police officers look on as Major General Stroop discusses razing the houses on Niska and Muranowska Streets with Kaleschke, his police adjutant. (*USHMM: National Archives*)

SS troops force Jewish labourers to evacuate a Warsaw ghetto factory during the uprising. (*USHMM: National Archives*)

A roll call of the members of the fire brigade in the Łódź ghetto. (USHMM: Robert Abrams)

Police line up for a roll call in the Łódź ghetto. (USHMM: Robert Abrams)

Four photographs showing a Jewish outdoor market in the Łódź ghetto. Due to the restrictions on currency, Jews would often trade furniture and clothing for food to survive. *(USHMM: Robert Abrams)*

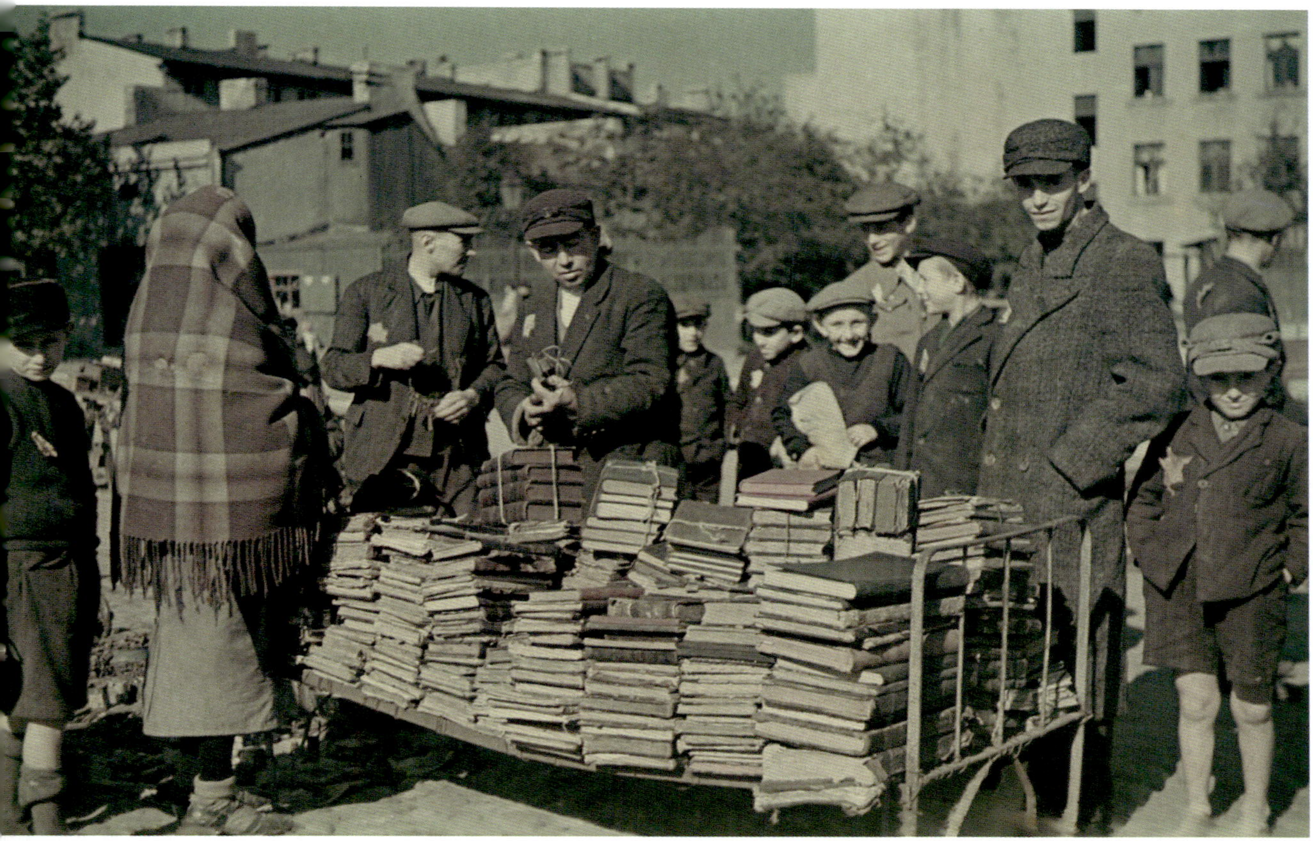

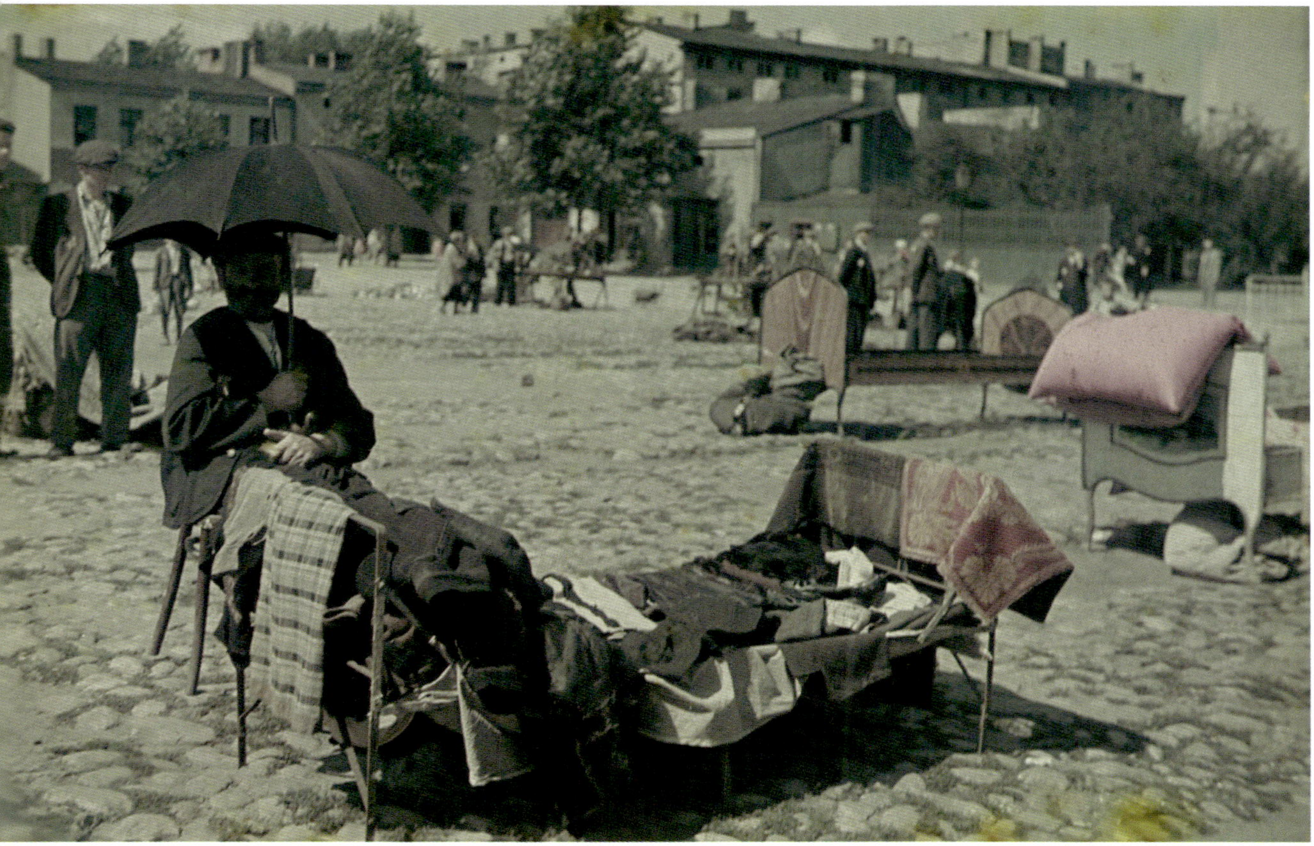

(**Above**) A market in the Łódź ghetto. On 30 April 1940 the Łódź ghetto was closed and segregated from the rest of the city. It housed some 163,777 residents, many of whom worked for the German war economy. The ghetto survived until August 1944. In the first two years it absorbed about 20,000 Jews from liquidated ghettos in nearby Polish towns and villages as well as areas in German-occupied Europe. The first liquidation actions began in early 1942, transporting Łódź residents to their deaths at Auschwitz and Chełmno extermination camps. It was the last ghetto in occupied Poland to be liquidated, and during its establishment some 210,000 Jews had been forced to live or die there. When the Russians arrived at the ghetto in August 1944, 877 were found still living there, hiding in buildings and cellars. (*USHMM: Robert Abrams*)

(**Opposite, above**) Women walk past a shop in the Łódź ghetto – there was also trading in shops. Orders prohibited any commercial exchange between Jews and non-Jews in Łódź, and to survive inside the ghetto it was important that you had something to trade. Money was exchanged, but the only legal currency in the ghetto was specially created called ghetto currency. (*USHMM: Robert Abrams*)

(**Opposite, below**) A typical street scene inside the Łódź ghetto. (*USHMM: Robert Abrams*)

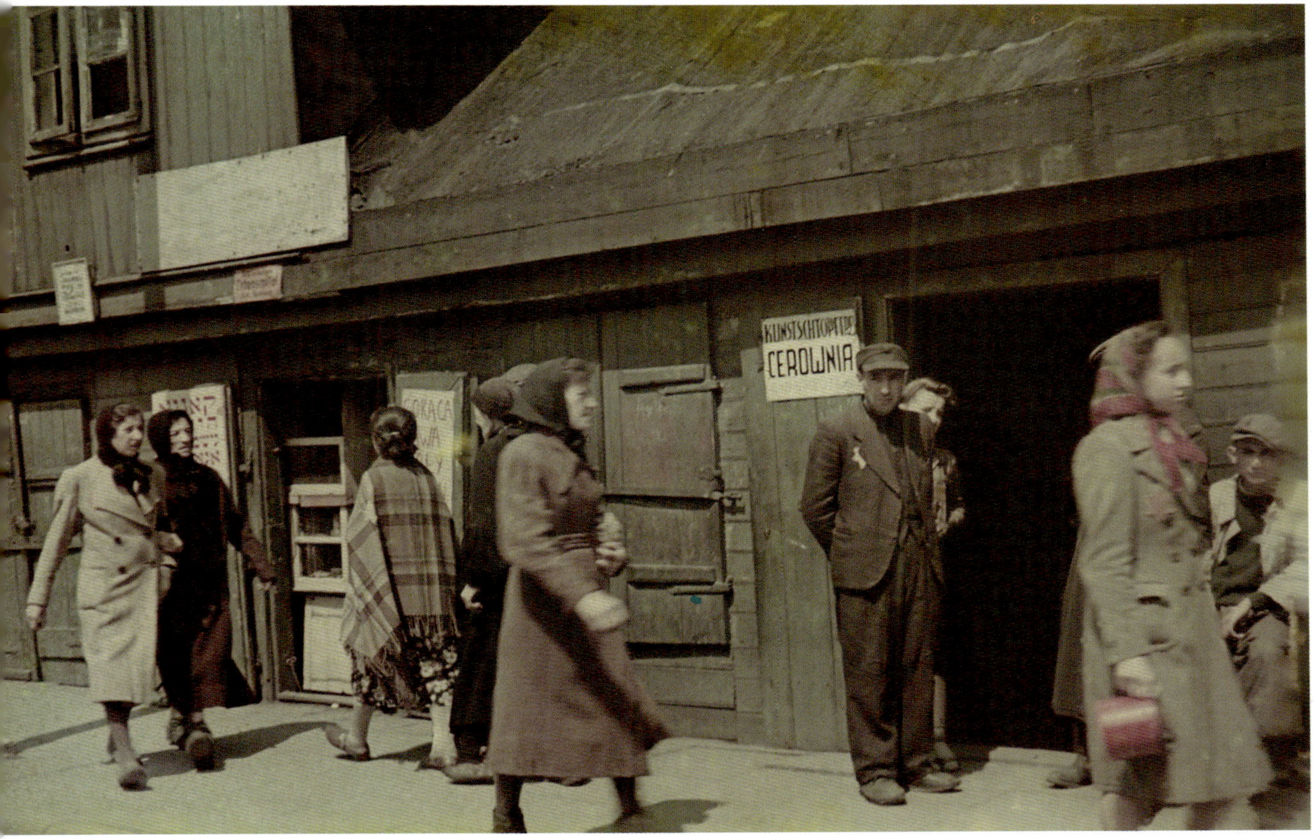
CEROWNIA

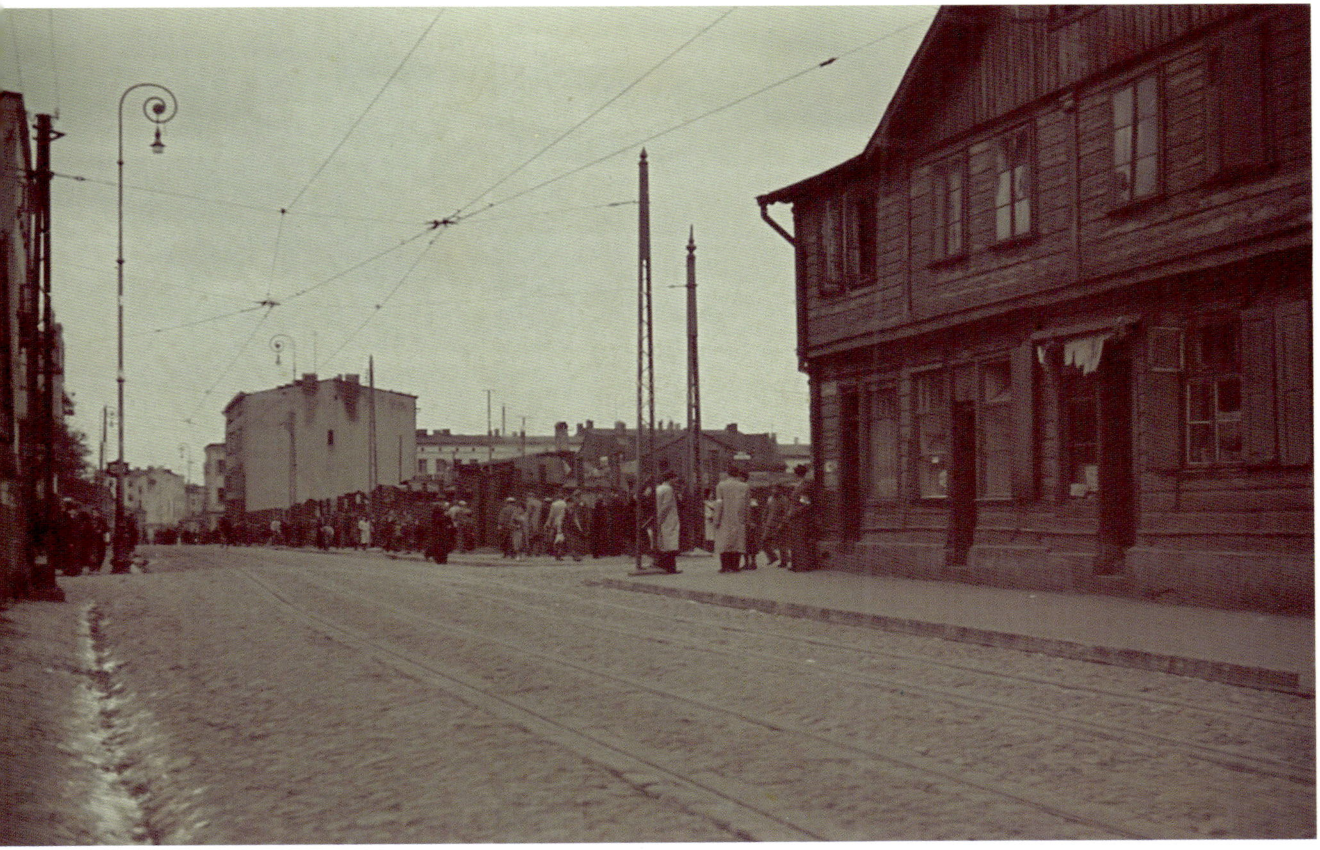

Some ghetto residents fill up watering cans with a hose on a street in the Łódź ghetto. Clean running water was at a premium inside the ghetto. *(USHMM: Robert Abrams)*

Ghetto schoolchildren holding small pails and cups wait in line outside the ghetto soup kitchen. *(USHMM: Robert Abrams)*

A view of the main street in the ghetto. (USHMM: Robert Abrams)

A smiling Hans Biebow, German head of the Łódź ghetto administration, observing an elderly and destitute Jew in the ghetto. From 1942, Biebow and his deputies Józef Haemmerle and Wilhelm Ribbe imposed ever harsher restrictions on ghetto life. (USHMM: Robert Abrams)

A man, who has removed his hat, walks down a street in the Łódź ghetto. A decree obliged Jews to wear a distinct Star of David. In the General Government, Jews wore a white armband with a blue Star of David; in the Warthegau, a yellow badge in the form of a Star of David on the left breast and on the back. If a Jew was found in public without the star he could be severely punished. (USHMM: Robert Abrams)

A group of ghetto residents congregate on a street of the Łódź ghetto. (USHMM: Robert Abrams)

Two men and a female nurse converse outside the furniture factory in the Łódź ghetto. *(USHMM: Robert Abrams)*

Izak Lewkowizc, a young ghetto postman, delivers mail or ration cards to the ghetto residents. *(USHMM: Robert Abrams)*

Hans Biebow, German administrator of the Łódź ghetto, talks to a group of Jewish women on the doorstep of a building in the Łódź ghetto. *(USHMM: Robert Abrams)*

German officials inspect a textiles storeroom in the Łódź ghetto. Hans Biebow and Mordechai Chaim Rumkowski, head of the Jewish Council, created an industrial base manufacturing war supplies in the ghetto. *(USHMM: Robert Abrams)*

Workers in the saddle-making workshop in the Łódź ghetto. Hans Biebow believed that the Jews would work hard to survive, and forced the Jewish population to work 12-hour days despite dreadful conditions. Work gangs produced clothing, metal and woodwork, and electrical equipment for the German military. *(USHMM: Robert Abrams)*

Woodworkers in the furniture factory in the Łódź ghetto. By 1943, according to Rumkowski, 95 per cent of the adult population of the ghetto was employed in 117 workshops. *(USHMM: Robert Abrams)*

Teenagers work in the Łódź ghetto metal workshop. Working in these factories were harsh and workers were entirely dependent on the Germans. (*USHMM: Robert Abrams*)

Workers manufacture wooden shoes in the Łódź ghetto. Conditions were so bad that workers sometimes went on strike. The Jewish Police would usually silence them, although in at least one instance the German Order Police had to intervene. (*USHMM: Robert Abrams*)

A bearded, religious, Jewish vendor stands by his stall in the Łódź ghetto. *(USHMM: Robert Abrams)*

Women work in the ghetto laundry. *(USHMM: Robert Abrams)*

Hans Biebow examines some ties for sale in the outdoor market of the Łódź ghetto. (USHMM: Robert Abrams)

Ghetto fire-fighters ride in the back of a fire truck through the Łódź ghetto. (USHMM: Robert Abrams)

In this photograph workers dispose of sewage in the Łódź ghetto. (USHMM: Robert Abrams)

A typical street scene in the Łódź ghetto. Children can be seen playing. (USHMM: Robert Abrams)

View of Łódź ghetto residents crossing the bridge over Zgierska Street at Koscielny Square. *(USHMM: Robert Abrams)*

A street scene in the Łódź ghetto. *(USHMM: Robert Abrams)*

Stroop (centre) accompanied by SS and police officers looks on as SS soldiers uncover the entrance to an underground bunker during the suppression of the Warsaw ghetto uprising. The original German caption reads: 'They were also discovered in underground bunkers.' (*USHMM: National Archives*)

SS troops force Jews to dig out the entrance to a bunker on the twentieth day of suppression of the uprising. The original German caption reads: 'A bunker is opened.' (*USHMM: National Archives*)

Jews captured during the suppression of the Warsaw ghetto uprising are marched to the Umschlagplatz for deportation. The original German caption reads: 'To the Umschlagplatz.' (*USHMM: National Archives*)

An SS soldier stands among ruins in the Warsaw ghetto. (*USHMM: National Archives*)

Again, captured Jews are marched to the Umschlagplatz for deportation. (*USHMM: National Archives*)

SS troops arrest the Jewish department heads of the Brauer armament factory during the Warsaw ghetto uprising. (*USHMM: National Archives*)

SS troops guard members of the Jewish resistance captured during the suppression of the Warsaw ghetto uprising. The original German caption reads: 'These bandits offered armed resistance.' (USHMM: National Archives)

An SS soldier searches a captured Jewish resistance fighter during the suppression of the Warsaw ghetto uprising. The original German caption reads: 'Pulled from a bunker.' (USHMM: National Archives)

An SS sergeant (*Oberscharführer*) interrogates religious Jews captured during the suppression of the Warsaw ghetto uprising. The original German caption reads: 'Jewish rabbis.' Among those pictured is Rabbi Heschel Rappaport. (*USHMM: National Archives*)

An SS lieutenant (*Untersturmführer*) interrogates a Jewish resistance fighter captured on the twenty-first day of the suppression of the Warsaw ghetto uprising. (*USHMM: Louis Gonda*)

Jews captured by SS and SD troops during the suppression of the Warsaw ghetto uprising are forced to leave their shelter and march to the Umschlagplatz for deportation. (USHMM: National Archives)

More Jews captured by the SS are marched to the Umschlagplatz for deportation. The original German caption reads: 'How the former Jewish residential quarter looks after its destruction.' (USHMM: National Archives)

An SS officer questions Jewish resistance fighters as Stroop (rear, centre) and his security detail look on. The original German caption reads: 'Jewish traitors.'
(USHMM: National Archives)

Jews captured by the SS during the Warsaw ghetto uprising are interrogated beside the ghetto wall before being sent to the Umschlagplatz. The original German caption reads: 'Search and Interrogation.' (USHMM: National Archives)

Jews captured by the SS during the suppression of the Warsaw ghetto uprising are lined up against a wall before being searched for weapons. The original German caption reads: 'Before the search.' (*USHMM: National Archives*)

SS troops and officers search the Jewish department heads of the Brauer armaments factory during the suppression of the Warsaw ghetto uprising. (*USHMM: National Archives*)

SS troops guard members of the Jewish resistance captured during the suppression of the Warsaw ghetto uprising. The original German caption reads: 'Bandits!' (*USHMM: National Archives*)

Jewish families surrender to the SS during the suppression of the Warsaw ghetto uprising. The original German caption reads: 'Smoking out the Jews and bandits.' (*USHMM: National Archives*)

SS troops search ruined buildings for survivors during the suppression of the uprising. (*USHMM: National Archives*)

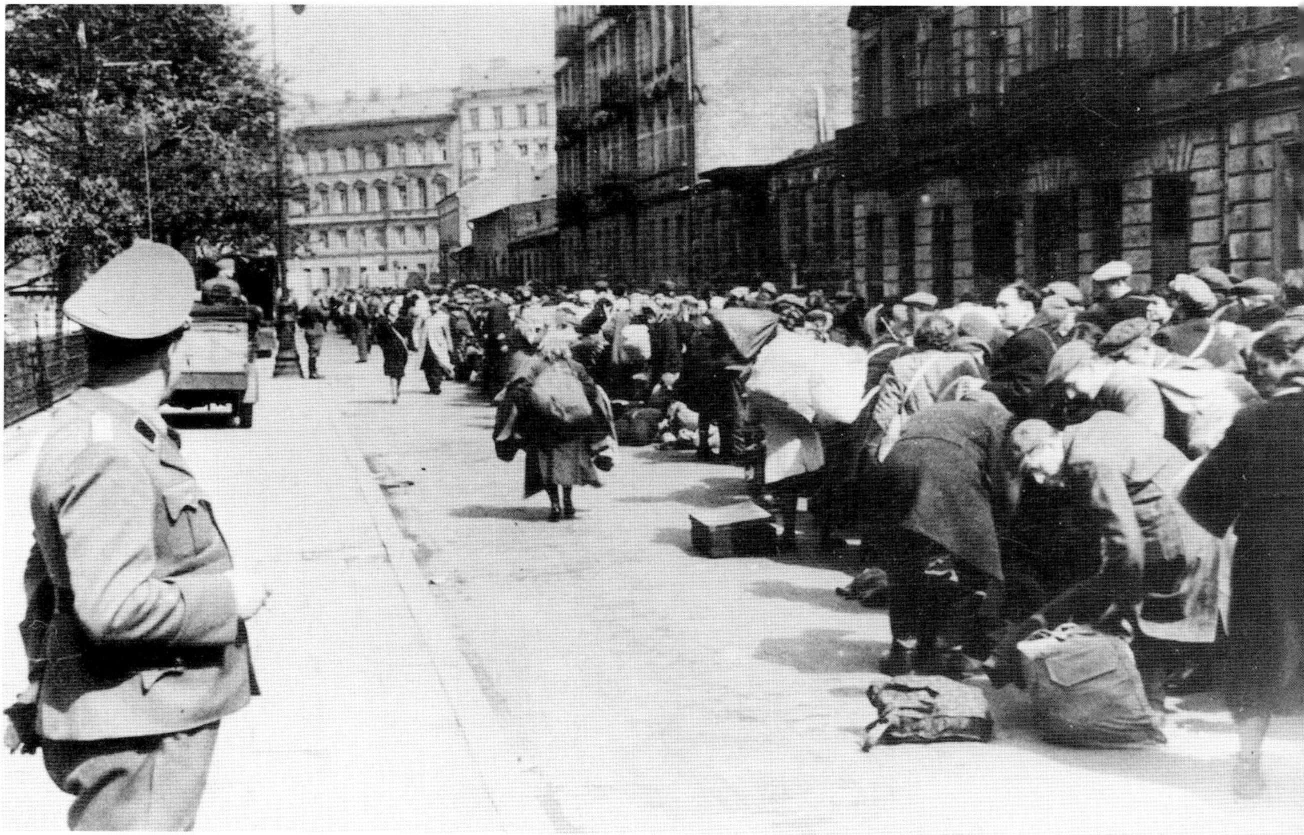

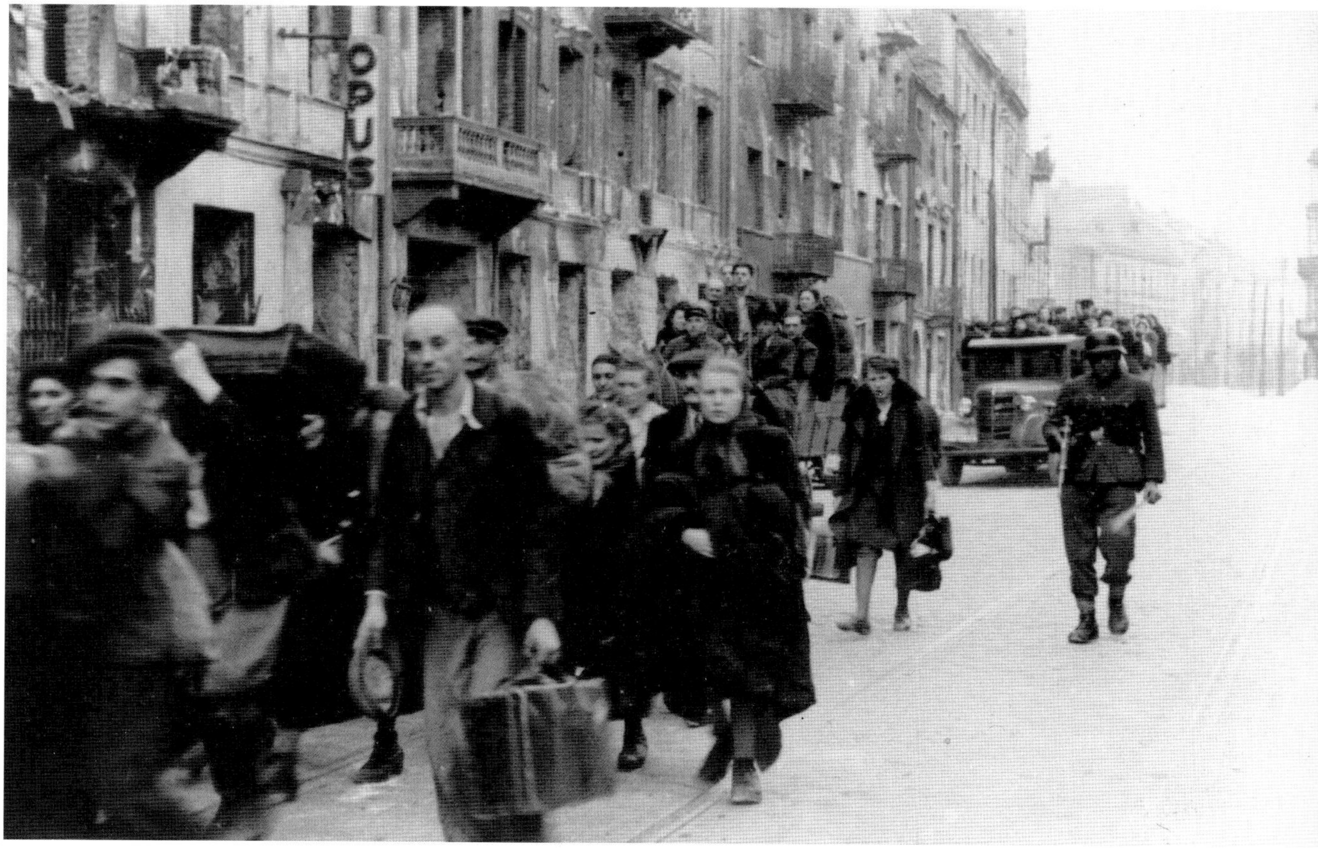
OPUS

(**Opposite, above**) An SS soldier oversees the deportation of survivors of the Warsaw ghetto uprising. This photo was one of a number of images taken of the deportation. It was commissioned by Friedrich Wilhelm Krueger, higher SS and police leader in Kraków, and bound in leather. The report was intended as a souvenir album for Heinrich Himmler to celebrate the hard-won victory of the Warsaw uprising. (*USHMM: George Bogart*)

(**Opposite, below**) Jews captured by the SS during the suppression of the Warsaw ghetto uprising march to the Umschlagplatz for deportation. (*USHMM: National Archives*)

(**Above**) Jews captured by the SS during the suppression of the Warsaw ghetto uprising are forced to board a truck that will likely take them to a labour camp. Most of the people captured during the ghetto uprising were deported to Treblinka; some were sent to Trawniki or to Poniatowa. (*USHMM: Leopold Page Photographic Collection*)

The Aftermath

By mid-1943, clearing of the ghettos in the General Government was virtually complete and the death camps were receiving the last deliveries. Apart from the last Jews from Warsaw, during this period the bulk of the shipments being received were now from Western Europe. Some of what the Nazis referred to as 'healthy stock' were still being put to work. Jews that had been left in the General Government were now transferred to labour camps where they were used in the war effort, being hired out to firms for cash on a daily basis, returning to the camps at night. SS-Reichsführer Heinrich Himmler, however, declared that the employment of Jews would cease, with the exception of highly skilled workers such as precision mechanics or qualified craftsmen. Himmler was by this time aware that the situation on the Eastern Front had deteriorated considerably, but even this did not diminish his determination to deport and murder of Jews. In fact so fanatical was he that he actually accelerated the deportations.

By 1944, almost all the ghettos had been 'cleansed' of Jews. A very few were still being used for labour, but virtually everyone else had been killed.

When the war ended in May 1945, some 3 million Polish Jews, half of all those killed during the Holocaust, were dead. The ghettos had contained some 2 million Jews, most of whom had been sent to the extermination camps, and many had died on the way. Those not sent to the various labour camps or death factories were murdered near their 'homes' in mass executions in secluded killing sites.

The ghettos of Poland had played a pivotal part in the Holocaust. To the Jewish inhabitants the ghettos were a temporary stopping point before being resettled. To the Germans the ghettos were a means of eradicating the Jewish population from Europe once and for all.

Appendix I

List of Polish Ghettos

It should be noted that not all temporary Polish ghettos are not listed here. Often permanent ghettos were created only in settlements with rail connections. There were at least another forty-five transient ghettos erected throughout Poland. The list below contains what the Nazi authorities selected as their main Polish designated ghetto areas. When transient ghettos were liquidated the surviving inhabitants were sometimes forced into the more permanent ghettos. However, there were many cases where the transient ghettos were liquidated and the inhabitants sent directly to the extermination camps, or simply murdered in the surrounding field or forests.

Baranowicz Ghetto

In 1939 following the invasion of Poland the Jewish population of 9,000 in the city was joined by approximately 3,000 Jewish refugees from the Polish areas occupied by the Wehrmacht in September 1939. Following the invasion of Russia the city was captured by German forces on 25 June 1941. It became part of *Generalbezirk Weißruthenien* in *Reichskommissariat Ostland* during the German occupation. Two months later, in August 1941, a ghetto was built in the city, with more than 12,000 Jews held in six buildings on the outskirts. From 4 March to 14 December 1942 the ghetto was liquidated and the entire Jewish population transported to various concentration camps where they were nearly all murdered. About 250 survived the war.

Będzin Ghetto

In July 1940 a ghetto was created in the town. Some 20,000 local Jews from Będzin along with an additional 10,000 from neighbouring areas were forced into the ghetto. All able-bodied people were forced to work in German military factories before the ghetto was finally liquidated. The inmates who had not died of disease, hunger or mistreatment were taken by train to the nearby concentration camp at Auschwitz and were exterminated. The last major deportation of the ghetto saw an uprising between 1 and 3 August 1943 by members of the Jewish Combat Organisation.

Bialystok Ghetto

This ghetto was ordered to be built between 26 July and early August 1941 in Bezirk Bialystok. Some 50,000 Jews from the city and surrounding areas were forced into a small area of the city. The ghetto was divided in two by the Biala River. Most

Będzin ghetto: A street scene showing the Będzin ghetto.

Bialystok ghetto: German soldiers surround a group of Jewish men who stand with their hands up in a public square in Bialystok. *(USHMM: Jerzy Tomaszewski)*

inhabitants were used as slave labour, primarily in large textile, shoe and chemical companies. In November 1943 the ghetto was finally liquidated and all its inhabitants transported to Majdanek and Treblinka extermination camps. A couple of hundred survived the war, either by hiding in the Polish sector of the city or escaping following the Bialystok ghetto uprising.

Brzesc Ghetto
The Brzesc ghetto was formed in December 1941. Approximately 20,000 inhabitants of the city including the communities in the surrounding area were forced into it. Within a year, between 15 and 18 October 1942, the ghetto was liquidated and all the inhabitants murdered. Some 5,000 Jews were forced out of the ghetto under the guise of being resettled but were executed nearby at the Brest Fortress; the remainder were killed by shooting squads inside the forest of Bronna Gora.

Buczacz Ghetto
The town of Buczacz came under German occupation on 7 July 1941 and within a few months established a *Judenräte*. By the end of 1942 the 4,500 Jews were either murdered or transported to Bełżec death camp. At this time a ghetto was established which was soon filled with refugees from nearby communities. By early April 1943 more than 2,000 Jews regarded as 'unskilled labour' were removed from the ghetto and murdered in pits near Fedor Hill. Soon after, more inmates inside the ghetto were removed and sent to the Podheitzka labour camp. In April and May 1943, an additional 3,000 Jews were murdered. By June 1943, the last of the ghetto was liquidated with Jews deported or shot.

Częstochowa Ghetto
The Częstochowa Ghetto was created on 8 April 1941, and within a year some 40,000 Jews were contained inside its boundaries. On 22 September 1942 the ghetto was ordered to be liquidated and most of the inhabitants were removed onto trains under the guise of resettlement but sent to Treblinka death camp. In June 1943 those still in the ghetto launched an uprising, but was soon stopped by the SS and everyone responsible was murdered.

Czortkow Ghetto
In early 1942, the Czortkow Ghetto was created to confine the Jewish population of the city and the surrounding areas between Rzeznicka, Składowa, Targowa, Lazienna, Podolska and Szkolna. On 26 August 1942, around 2,500 Jews from the ghetto were deported to Bełżec death camp, including 500 children, their mothers and the sick.

Drohobych Ghetto
In July 1941, the Drohobych ghetto was formed and became a large open-type ghetto holding around 10,000 Jews. The first part of its liquidation took place in late

Częstochowa ghetto: View of Rynek Warszawski Square in Częstochowa, where Jews in the ghetto were assembled for forced labour and deportation. (*USHMM: Biblioteka Publiczna w Częstochowie*)

Drohobych ghetto: The inhabitants moving from one part of the ghetto to another with their possessions in sacks.

March 1942 with the deportation of 2,000 inmates who were sent directly to the Bełżec extermination camp. The next deportation lasted for nine days in 8–17 August 1942 with 2,500 herded onto trains and sent away to be murdered. Another 600 were killed in and around the ghetto trying to hide or escape. The ghetto was closed down in late September 1942.

Grodno Ghetto

The Grodno ghetto was erected in November 1941. It was divided into two areas, one in the old part of the city around the synagogue: 15,000 Jews were forced to live in this area. The other was established in the Slobodka suburb, with 10,000 Jews living in this district. The division of the ghettos was undertaken purposely by German administration to facilitate the liquidation the ghettos more easily. The larger ghetto was liquidated in November 1943, the smaller one a few months earlier. Most of the Jews from Grodno were either murdered by mass shootings or marched off to the Sammellager in Kiełbasin to be deported to Auschwitz-Birkenau. By order of the SS before their deportation some Jews were ordered to sign postcards in German that read, 'Being treated well, we are working and everything is fine.'

Grodno ghetto: Under police supervision, Jews move their belongings into the ghetto. *(USHMM: Jacob Igra)*

Izbica Ghetto

The Izbica ghetto was created to serve as a transfer point for deportation of Jews from Poland, German, Austria and Czechoslovakia. It was created in March and April 1941, but the ghetto was not closed off at this time, with the Jews remaining within the restricted area near the main railway line. Because the ghetto was a special transit area, to make additional space for the incoming transports some 2,200 Jews were sent to the Bełżec death camp on 24 March 1942. Between March and May 1942, 12,000–15,000 Jews were transported to Izbica from across Europe. The liquidation of ghetto began on 2 November 1942. Around 4,500 Jews were forced out of Izbica and marched by the Sonderdienst battalion of Ukrainian Trawnikis and killed in mass pits. A second, smaller ghetto was hastily erected where the former ghetto was established. Some 1,000 local Jews were contained there until it was finally liquidated on 28 April 1943 with all the surviving inmates sent to the Sobibor death camp.

Kielce Ghetto

The Kielce Ghetto was created on 31 March 1941 and was surrounded by high fences of barbed wire. Eighty-five guards from Police Battalion 305 guarded the

Izbica ghetto: Slave labourers carrying wicker cases containing ammunition for the German army inside the ghetto.

Kielce ghetto: A group of children from a ghetto orphanage standing on the street. (*USHMM: Rafal Imbro*)

perimeter. The ghetto was split in two parts. During the following months the population of the ghetto expanded until in August 1942 there was estimated to be 27,000 Jews packed inside it. During this period the SS opened a number of forced-labour enterprises, including the Hasag Grant Werke which manufactured munitions, and a large woodworking plant, plus a number of other workshops. The liquidation of the ghetto, in three phases over five days, began on 20 August 1942: phase one was murdering the sick, disabled and elderly; phase two was rounding up 6,500 women and children, herding them onto Okrzei Street and transporting them to the Treblinka extermination camp. The last phase consisted of liquidating the rest of the ghetto by killing 1,200 patients in the Jewish hospital and then force-marching around 20,000 onto trains bound for Treblinka death camp. By 24 August 1942 there were still 2,000 Jews remaining in the ghetto, as these were required for the German war effort in the factories. It was not until September 1943 that the slave labour facilities were abandoned and the remaining workers sent to Auschwitz and Buchenwald to either work or die.

Kolomja Ghetto

In the summer of 1941 the town of Kolomja was captured by the Germans during the invasion of Russia. Under German occupation most of the city's Jews were murdered, some 500 in street executions. The following year the remaining Jews were massed in a local ghetto, and during the liquidation of the ghetto they were sent to various camps including Bełżec. A few hundred survived the transportation and were kept as slave workers, and then murdered in 1943 in a forest.

Kolomja ghetto: Jews inside the ghetto in the summer of 1941.

Końskowola Ghetto

The Końskowola ghetto was established in the town in 1941; many of its inmates were relocated Slovakian Jews. On 8 May 1942 some of them were transported to the Sobibor extermination camp. In October 1942 Reserve Police Battalion 101 carried out a massacre of some 800–1,000: the terrified inhabitants were taken to a nearby forest and murdered. The ghetto's remaining inmates were transferred to another camp.

Kraków Ghetto

Following the expulsion of 23,000 Jews from Kraków in 1940, a year later on 3 March 1941 the establishment of the Kraków ghetto was ordered. It was established in the Pódgorze District in April and was soon enclosed by a wall made of barbed wire and stone. The stones used were designed to look like tombstones, and Jewish monuments and tombstones from the cemetery were also used for the construction. Initially it was populated by 16,000 Jews and divided into two parts: Ghetto 'A' was for the work force, Ghetto 'B' for the rest. This division was for the ease of the

Końskowola ghetto: A German soldier patrols a street in the ghetto with his dog. (*USHMM: Instytut Pamieci Narodowej*)

Kraków ghetto: Jews are assembled for deportation. (*USHMM: Archiwum Dokumentacji Mechanicznej*)

liquidation of the ghetto, which began in stages from 30 May 1942 onwards. The first transport consisted of 7,000 Jews, the second 4,000, all to Bełżec on 5 June 1942. The final liquidation of the ghetto was carried on 13 and 14 March 1943. Those deemed unfit for labour, around 2,000, were rounded up and either murdered in the streets or transported to Auschwitz. The 8,000 that were left were transported and forced to work in the Płaszów labour camp.

Lachwa Ghetto

On 1 April 1942, the town's Jewish residents were forcibly moved into a new ghetto, known as the Lachwa ghetto, which comprised two streets and forty-five houses and was surrounded by a barbed-wire fence. The ghetto housed some 2,500 people. By September 1942, five months after the establishment of the ghetto, Lachwa was ordered to be liquidated. On 2 September, 150 German troops from the *Einsatzgruppe* killing squad, with 200 Belarusian and Ukrainian auxiliaries, surrounded the ghetto. When they moved in, there was an uprising among a Polish and Jewish resistance group which resulted in approximately 650 Jews being killed in the fighting. Some 500 were taken prisoner, escorted to nearby pits and shot. During the uprising the ghetto fence was breached and around 1,000 Jews were able to escape, with about 600 of them hiding in the surrounding marshes. Most of the escapers were caught and shot, but 120 managed to escape and join a resistance group.

Lida Ghetto

In December 1941 the Lida ghetto was created in the suburbs of the town. Five months later, on 7 May 1942, the ghetto was ordered for liquidation and sealed off by guards and auxiliaries. The following day, nearly 6,000 were forced out of ghetto and taken to a nearby military firing range where they were shot in grave pits. Some 1,500 educated Jews remained in the ghetto, and the population was added to by incoming refugees. A few groups secretly escaped and hid in the surrounding forests until the city was liberated in 9 July 1944, but the remaining occupants of the Lida ghetto and neighbouring areas were killed on 18 September 1943.

Łódź ghetto

By 1 February 1940 the relocation of the Łódź Jews into the newly-established Łódź ghetto was completed in the north-eastern part of city. Approximately 160,000 Jews from the city were crammed into the ghetto and the area was isolated from the rest of Łódź with barbed-wire fencing. The ghetto was divided in to three sections by the intersection of two major roads. By January 1942 the first stages of the liquidation of the ghetto began with 70,000 Jews being deported to the Chełmno killing centre. Then there were no more deportations until May 1944 when some 3,000 were sent to Chełmno. Three months later, all the surviving residents were sent to Auschwitz-Birkenau.

Łódź ghetto: Street scene inside the ghetto. *(USHMM: Jerzy Tomaszewski)*

Łomża Ghetto

The Łomża Ghetto was erected on 12 August 1941. Between 10,000 and 18,000 Jews were forced to live in a small area of the town. The ghetto was liquidated on 1 November 1942 when all the residents were forced out of their squalid dwellings and required to march to a railway line where they were transported to Auschwitz-Birkenau for extermination.

Lubartów Ghetto

Lubartów ghetto was established from 1941 until October 1942. Polish Jews were initially confined there, but eventually neighbouring communities full of Jews were sent to the ghetto, including the large towns of Lublin and Ciechanow, totalling around 3,500. In May 1942, additional transports of Slovakian Jews were sent there. There were several stages in its liquidation, the first on 9 April 1942. On the first day, 800 Jews who did not have work cards were transported to the Bełżec extermination camp. On 11 October the final part of the liquidation of the ghetto took place with 3,000 Jews being sent to Bełżec, Majdanek and Treblinka.

Lublin Ghetto

The Lublin Ghetto was erected in March 1941. It contained mainly Polish Jews, but there were some transports of Roma inhabitants too. Between mid-March and mid-April 1942 during the ghettos liquidation over 30,000 Jews were sent to Bełżec and 4,000 to Majdanek, where they were murdered.

Łomża ghetto: One of the Jewish Ghetto Police or Jewish Police Service (*Jüdische Ghetto-Polizei* or *Jüdischer Ordnungsdienst*) can be seen at one of the entrances to the ghetto in the summer of 1942. These auxiliary police units were organized within the ghettos by local Jewish councils or *Judenrat*.

Lublin ghetto: German soldiers watch Jewish women shop at the outdoor market of the ghetto.
(USHMM: Evan Bukey)

Łuck Ghetto

The Łuck ghetto was established by the German occupying authorities in December 1941 with a population of some 20,000 people. It began its liquidation on 19 August 1942. Some 17,000 Jews were rounded up by units of the Order Police Battalions and the Ukrainian Auxiliary Police and taken in batches by lorry to the Gorka Polonka forest on the outskirts of the town. There were many women and children and all were shot in prepared trenches. The final liquidation of the ghetto began on 12 December 1942, but the remaining Jews had barricaded themselves inside a school and determined to fight to the death. They were all killed.

Lwow Ghetto

On 8 November 1941 the Lwow ghetto was established in the northern part of the city and all Poles and Ukrainians living there were ordered to move out. They were replaced with some 80,000 Jews by 15 December 1941. During the first months of 1942 an additional 30,000 Jews were forced into the already cramped ghetto. Between 16 March and 1 April 1942 the German authorities began liquidating the ghetto with some 15,000 Jews deported to the Bełżec extermination camp. A few months later through August a further 40,000 or 50,000 Jews were rounded up and sent to Bełżec. In early January 1943 another 15,000–20,000 were forced outside the

Lwow ghetto: Execution by hanging of members of the ghetto *Judenrat*. (*USHMM: Herman Lewinter*)

town and shot with the last members of the *Judenräte* hanged. At the beginning of June 1943 the Germans announced that the ghetto was finally 'cleansed' of its inhabitants.

Marcinkance Ghetto

In November 1941 a small ghetto in the town of Marcinkance was erected near the Saint Petersburg–Warsaw railway station. Some 320 Jews were forced to live there in a number of houses. A year later, on 2 November 1942, orders were given to liquidate the ghetto and transport the Jews to Treblinka and Auschwitz.

Miedzyrzec Ghetto

In 1940 the Germans set up the Miedzyrzec ghetto in the historic neighbourhood of Szmulowizna. This ghetto was regarded as a transit ghetto to hold 20,000 Jews. Eventually it became the main transit ghetto in the northern part of the Lublin district. From here the Jews were transported to the Treblinka death camp. On 25-26 August 1942, half of the ghetto was liquidated with 11,000–12,000 Jews rounded up by German Order Police Battalions and deported to Treblinka.

Miedzyrzec ghetto: Police with auxiliary personnel in the ghetto, probably in 1942. (ARC)

Minsk ghetto: This warning sign actually hung on the fence of the 'Gross-K-Werk Minsk', a large forced-labour enterprise of the Daimler-Benz Company in Minsk. (*USHMM: Belarusian State Museum of the History of the Great Patriotic War*)

Minsk Ghetto
The Minsk ghetto was established on 25 October 1940. Some 5,000 Jews were forced to relocate there from all over the city, and over the coming weeks and months it expanded with Jews being brought in from neighbouring areas. On 21 August 1942 the ghetto was liquidated with some 5,000 Jews being forced out of their squalid living quarters onto freight trains bound for Treblinka.

Mizocz Ghetto
Following the German invasion of Russia in the summer of 1941, the Mizocz ghetto was erected. The following year, in October, the ghetto was liquidated. However, the 1,700 inhabitants fought back. The uprising lasted only a couple of days. On 14 October the captured survivors were herded onto lorries and transported to a nearby ravine where they were stripped of their clothing and executed.

Mizocz ghetto: A German police officer shoots Jewish women who are still alive after a mass execution of Jews from the Mizocz ghetto. According to the Zentrale Stelle in Germany (Zst. II 204 AR 1218/70), these Jews were collected by the German Gendarmerie and Ukrainian *Schutzmannschaft* during the liquidation of the Mizocz ghetto, which held around 1,700 Jews. On the eve of the ghetto's liquidation (13 October 1942), some of the inhabitants rose up against the Germans and were defeated after a short battle. The remaining members of the community were transported from the ghetto to this ravine in the Sdolbunov Gebietskommissariat, south of Rovno, where they were executed. *(USHMM: Instytut Pamieci Narodowej)*

Nowogrodek Ghetto

On 22 February 1942 an order was announced to create the Nowogrodek ghetto. Some 4,500 Jews were forced to live in the ghetto which was erected around the synagogue and within the streets of Łysogórska and Słonimska. Within a couple of months parts of the ghetto were ordered to be liquidated and this commenced with first arresting and murdering members of the *Judenräte*. This followed with about 1,200 Jews being forced out of the town and marched to the Kurpiasz Forest where they were all shot in hastily prepared pits. On 6 August 1942, the final part of the liquidation of the ghetto took place with another massacre. Some 2,000–3,000 Jews were executed into mass graves in the Jewish cemetery on the southern outskirts of Zdzięcioł.

Nowy Sacz Ghetto

The Nowy Sacz ghetto was ordered to be established in June 1941 and was erected into two interconnected parts of the city centre. Some 12,000 Jews were forced to relocate there. Over a year its final liquidation took place starting from 23 August 1942. Under the pretence that it was a 'resettlement in the East', it lasted three days. It is estimated that 15,000 Jews were removed from the ghetto and transported to the Bełżec extermination camp.

Nowy Sacz ghetto: Polish Jews wearing armbands walk down a street in the ghetto. (*USHMM: Michael O'Hara*)

Opatow ghetto: Majer Sztajman poses on a cobblestone street in the ghetto, holding his baby daughter Mania. *(USHMM: Marion Weinzweig)*

Opatów Ghetto

The Opatów ghetto was erected in 1940 and was initially an open-type ghetto with around 7,000 people crammed into a small area. On 13 May 1942 the ghetto was ordered to be closed off with fencing and barbed wire in preparation for its liquidation. Several months later, on 20 October, 6,500 Jewish men, women and children were rounded up in the centre of the town at Targowica Square. They were then marched 11 miles to the railway station stop in Jasice and transported to the Treblinka death camp. Some 2,000 slave labourers remained, but the following year they were removed to other work in other camps. The ghetto was then completely liquidated.

Pinsk Ghetto

On 20 April 1942 the Pinsk ghetto was established and the population soon grew to some 16,000 inhabitants. The ghetto's operation only lasted some six months when orders came through to liquidate it. Some 3,500 Jews were removed from the ghetto and marched to Kobryn where they were massacred. The final liquidation of the ghetto began on 28 October 1942, and in spite a small uprising, all the remaining inhabitants were murdered.

Pinsk ghetto: Himmler (centre) confers with SS and Police Leader Hans Adolf Pruetzmann (extreme left) and Ludolf Herman von Alvensleben (second from the left) during a visit to the Crimea. During this visit, Himmler gave Pruetzmann a written order to kill all the residents of the Pinsk Ghetto. (*USHMM: James Blevins*)

Piotrków Ghetto

The Piotrków ghetto was the first wartime ghetto of its kind and was established in late January 1940. Eventually some 28,000 Jews were crammed into a part of town where only 6,000 people had previously lived. It was not until 13 October 1942 that the ghetto liquidation began, with about 1,000 Jews being shot. By the next morning, around 22,000 were herded into the square for a 'selection'. What followed was a series of transportations to Majdanek and Treblinka death camps. Around 3,000 slave labour workers remained until they were eventually sent to Buchenwald and Ravensbrück concentration camps.

Radom Ghetto

The Radom ghetto was erected in March 1941 and operated until August 1942. During its liquidation some 31,000 men, women and children were removed from the ghetto and forced on trains to the Treblinka death camp where they were all murdered.

Sambor Ghetto

The Sambor ghetto was established in March 1942, with Jews from different parts of the city along with some inhabitants of neighbouring communities. The liquidation of the ghetto began on 2 August 1942 with 6,000 men, women and children being

Piotrków ghetto: Jewish women and children are gathered outside a wooden barracks in Piotrków Kujawski. (USHMM: Yad Vashem)

Radom ghetto: Jews forced into a small ghetto at Glinice in Radom. (*USHMM: Muzeum Okręgowe w Radomiu*)

rounded up and deported to Bełżec death camp. In the second stage, on 17 October, 3,500 were sent to Bełżec. A month later, on 17 November 1942, mass shootings of Jews were carried out. In early January 1943, the 1,500 workers that were left were rounded up, transported to various woods nearby, and murdered.

Siedlce Ghetto

The creation of the Siedlce ghetto was pronounced on 2 August 1941. It consisted of several small blocks and streets in the city centre north of the old square. On 1 October 1941 it was formally closed off to the outside world by a barbed-wire fence with three gates leading out. On 22 August 1942, the ghetto was ordered to be liquidated and 10,000 Jews were forced into the square. Approximately 500 were selected for work detail, the remainder were either murdered in pits outside the city or deported to Treblinka in railcars. By late November the remaining workers had been shot.

Słonim Ghetto

The Słonim ghetto was established in July 1941. The first part of its liquidation began almost immediately: Einsatzkommando 8 rounded up 2,000 Jews, transported them to specially prepared burial pits on the outskirts of the village, and murdered them. This made space for others. The second liquidation began on 14 November 1941 with another mass murder, this time by Einsatzgruppe B. Some 9,000 people were taken to the village of Czepielów where they were shot in the pits with rifles. Around

Siedlce ghetto: Jews are led through the streets of Siedlce on their way to the railway station during a deportation action from the ghetto. *(USHMM: Instytut Pamieci Narodowej)*

7,000 workers now remained, and in June 1942 they revolted. Fierce reprisals followed, leading to the ghetto's complete destruction between 29 June and 15 July 1942. Further murders continued in the surrounding communities. It is estimated that some 55,000 Jews had been murdered in the Słonim ghetto, including in the towns, villages, forests and fields that surrounded it, by August 1942.

Sosnowiec Ghetto

This ghetto was formed in 1942, and deportation actions were organised from the start with the help of the *Judenräte* in the selection of healthy men for the slave labour camps. Transfers took place in May, June and October 1942 involving some 3,500 Jews. In January 1943 the ghetto was moved to the Środula district, which bordered the Będzin ghetto. At this time there were some 13,000 Jews living in Sosnowiec ghetto. Six months later, in June 1943, the ghetto was liquidated and a deportation action saw most of the inhabitants transported to Auschwitz. The few hundred that remained in the Środula ghetto were murdered in January 1944.

Stanisławów Ghetto

The Stanisławów ghetto was established in December 1941 with some 20,000 Jews being contained behind brick walls and barbed-wire fences. In March 1942 the ghetto

Sosnowiec ghetto: Sewing workshop in ghetto. Seated in the middle is Hinda Chilewicz. Standing from the right is Dorka Piorko, Fredka Landau and Cesia Chmielnicka. Standing on the left is Mania Herszlikiewicz.
(*USHMM: William and Helen Luksenburg*)

Stanisławów ghetto: A guard at one of the entrances to the ghetto in the summer of 1942.

was ordered to be reduced in size after German and Ukrainian guards made a punishment raid for the council's non-compliance with its first deportation order. This involved burning down some buildings in the ghetto, and beating and murdering a number of Jews. In April, September and November 1942, there were deportations to the Bełżec death camp. Between 22 and 23 February 1943 the final liquidation was ordered and police forces surrounded the ghetto. The deportation action lasted four days. Most of the Jews were forced to the cemetery and shot, including the Jewish council. Soon after it was declared that the ghetto had been liquidated.

Stryj Ghetto

In late 1942 the Stryj ghetto was sealed off from the rest of the town and the Jews there lived in cramped and squalid conditions. During the ghetto's existence there were regular raids in which Jews were taken in small groups to the Holobotow forest for execution. In March 1943 the ghetto was ordered to be liquidated. Many inhabitants were shot inside the ghetto; those that were left, approximately 2,600, were taken to the Holobotow forest where they were ordered to undress, and murdered by gun fire.

Tarnopol Ghetto

In September 1941 the German occupation authorities designated a new Jewish ghetto around the old square and the market square of the metropolitan area of Tarnopol. Approximately 12,500 Jews were contained in it. The first liquidation began on 31 August 1942. Some 3,500 Jews were rounded up, locked in cattle cars, and transported, with another 3,000 Jews from the ghettos of Zbaraz and Mikulince, to the Bełżec death camp. The next deportation began on 10 November 1942, with around 2,500 Jews sent to Bełżec. The ghetto area was then greatly reduced and turned into a labour camp. In 1943 the remaining labourers were murdered, although a few hundred managed to escape death by hiding in the town.

Tarnów Ghetto

The Tarnów ghetto was officially established in March 1941. In June, Jews from the neighbouring area were moved into it and the population of the ghetto rose to approximately 40,000. In October 1942, the ghetto was split into Sections A and B. Section A was used primarily for forced labour and was divided into a male and a female division. Section B contained Jews that did not work. They were forbidden to move sections. Within a few days of dividing the ghetto, 2,500 Jews from Section B were herded into the city square. They were then marched to the station, and freighted to the Bełżec death camp. The ghetto would be finally liquidated in early September 1943 with some 6,000 being sent to Auschwitz to be what the Germans called 'processed'. Those remaining in the ghetto were later either killed or sent to the Płaszów labour camp.

Tarnopol ghetto: A German stands guard on a snow-covered railway track as a group of Jews are led to a deportation train.

Tarnów ghetto: Jews on a street in Tarnów shortly after the German invasion. (*USHMM: Valerie Rollins*)

Trochenbrod Ghetto

The Trochenbrod ghetto was established soon after the German invasion of Russia in June 1941. It operated for just over a year and was finally liquidated in August and September 1942 in a series of massacres by Order Police battalions. It was estimated that some 5,000 Jews were murdered from the ghetto and communities from the surrounding neighbourhood.

Vilna Ghetto

At the end of August 1941 the Vilna ghetto was established in the old Jewish quarter of the city where thousands of Jews were already living. It was estimated that some 70,000 Jews were crammed into it. During its operation until January 1942, task groups of German and Lithuanian *Einsatzgruppen* regularly carried out surprise operations called *Aktionen*, often on Jewish holidays. These involved round-ups in which the Jews were either executed within the ghetto limits or deported. Between late January and March 1943 ghetto life stabilized despite the horrendous living conditions. However, by August 1943 an order authorised its liquidation. This began with

Vilna ghetto: Jewish and Lithuanian police guard the entrance to the ghetto. *(USHMM: William Begell)*

the deportation of some 7,000 Jews to the Vaivara concentration camp in Estonia. The final phase of the liquidation of the ghetto came on 23 September 1943 when all the remaining residents were either sent to Vaivara, other death camps in Poland, or were killed in the forest of Paneriai.

Warsaw ghetto

The Warsaw ghetto was the largest of all the Jewish ghettos, not only in Poland but in all of occupied Europe. It was established in November 1940 and at its height as many as 460,000 Jews were held there within its brick walls. In summer 1942 the first part of the ghetto was liquidated with a massive deportation action involving some 265,000 ghetto residents. Most were sent to the newly opened Treblinka extermination camp, 20,000 were sent to labour camps. This took eight to twelve weeks to achieve, during which it became apparent to the Jews left inside the ghetto that these were deportations to death camps. A ghetto uprising followed in April 1943 which raged for a number of weeks with some 2,000 Waffen-SS troops sent in to eradicate the resistance groups. The ghetto was almost entirely levelled during the uprising. By 16 May 1943 the uprising had been quashed and the survivors, numbering about 50,000, were sent to either death or labour camps. Those that had not revolted in the uprising were also sent to labour camps or murdered, finally eradicating the ghetto.

Warsaw ghetto: Jews move along a crowded street in the ghetto. (*USHMM: Simon Adelman*)

Zdzięcioł Ghetto

The German authorities officially created Zdzięcioł ghetto for all local Jews on 22 February 1942. Over 4,500 were ordered to move there. On 29 April 1942 the liquidation of the ghetto was authorised. The first phase began with 1,200 Jews being forced to the southern edge of the town where they were murdered into specially prepared pits. The second phase began on 6 August 1942 and lasted for three days. Many Jews hid in prepared dugouts. During this action some 3,500 Jews were executed into three mass graves in the Jewish cemetery on the southern outskirts of the town.

Appendix II

Reserve Police Battalions 101

Police Battalion 101 was subordinated to the SS. It was initially given the task of guarding Polish PoWs behind German lines in 1939, then it was deployed in German-occupied areas, specifically the Army Group rear areas and territories under German civilian administration. The police units were given orders to target the civilian population throughout the General Government and were to carry out the expulsion of Poles from the Reichsgau Wartheland under the new Lebensraum policies. These expulsions were known as 'resettlement actions'. Police Battalion 101 operated in the new Warthegau territory around the cities of Łódź and Poznań. It was at the Łódź ghetto that the battalion was given duties to police the ghetto. Between June 1942 and November 1943 the battalion was assigned to support the liquidation of the ghetto, which consisted of not only assisting in their transportation to the extermination camps, but murdering them as well in mass shootings. They were also ordered to remove the Jews, with the aid of Trawnikis, from the Lublin, Izbica, Zamosc, Krasnik, Lomazy, Parczew, Miedzyrzec, Radzyn, Lukow, Konskowola, Tomaszow, Serokomla, and Kock ghettos.

Notes